Albert Clayton Applegarth

Quakers in Pennsylvania

Albert Clayton Applegarth

Quakers in Pennsylvania

ISBN/EAN: 9783337401771

Printed in Europe, USA, Canada, Australia, Japan

Cover: Foto ©Lupo / pixelio.de

More available books at **www.hansebooks.com**

JOHNS HOPKINS UNIVERSITY STUDIES

IN

HISTORICAL AND POLITICAL SCIENCE

HERBERT B. ADAMS, Editor

History is past Politics and Politics present History—*Freeman*

TENTH SERIES

VIII-IX

QUAKERS IN PENNSYLVANIA

By ALBERT C. APPLEGARTH, Ph. D.

BALTIMORE
THE JOHNS HOPKINS PRESS
August and September, 1892

QUAKERS IN PENNSYLVANIA.

I.

Quaker Customs.

Many centuries have been buried in the oblivion of the past since Pindar made his famous declaration that "custom is the king of all men." Although its author has long since passed away, succeeding ages have attested the correctness of the principle thus formulated. It is universally recognized that custom dominates the world of the present day; and it has to be conceded that it occupied a position of equal pre-eminence in the 17th century—at the period, when the Society of Friends emerged from obscurity, and attained a clear cut, well-defined existence. Although the adherence to their peculiar practices was primarily the cause of their persecution, yet bribes or tortures proved equally unavailing to induce them to relinquish their approved forms of speech, or to change their manner of life.

The Quakers were quick to perceive the vanity underlying most of the customs and habits prevalent in their day; hence their determined opposition. By this sect, Christianity was regarded as a heavenly dispensation; consequently its adherents contended that their faith should liberate them from the ostentation, insidious ceremonies, and other frivolities, unfortunately so common at that period.

For titles, and worldly honors generally, the Society always entertained special aversion. Its members strenuously refused to render any obeisance whatever to any distinctions of rank or honor. An instance is on record where William Penn was once accosted as *Lord* Penn in the Colony of Pennsylvania. To evidence their great displeasure at such unwarrantable procedure, the Assembly promptly ordered the practice to be discontinued, and a fine was imposed on the transgressor, presumably to stimulate his memory in the future. When addressing King Charles II, Penn never referred to him as "His Majesty," but always as "*Friend Charles;*" and the monarch, either in his characteristic spirit of levity or mockery, styled the son of the admiral, "Friend William." This principle also regulated their intercourse with the provincial authorities, who were always addressed in the plain and unvarnished language of Quakerism. The Friends, however, in this respect, were occasionally compelled to make some slight concessions. For example, when a formal petition was to be presented to the Crown, of course the usual phraseology had to be employed. But, in such cases, the majority of the Assembly were ever careful to pacify their consciences by appending to each address a declaration proclaiming that, although its substance received their approval, yet they "excepted against some of its style."

The Quakers even discarded the use of the ordinary Master or Sir in conversation and correspondence. A writer, who allows himself to become indignant over what he regards as such an insignificant matter, declares, "though they will not call anybody Sir or Master, they call everybody 'Friend,' although it is evident that, to a stranger, this must be mere civility, like the words they reject, and to an enemy, must approach nearly to insincerity." The Friends, however, were fortified in their position by what they apprehended to be the irrefragable teaching of the Scriptures, hence they continued steadfast in their opposition to the established custom. They contended that the Bible nowhere contained any such expressions as "My Lord Peter," or "My Lord Paul," consequently they agreed that all titles were to be promiscuously rejected. The Quakers, declares Penn, "affirm it to be sinful to give flattering titles, or to use vain gestures and compliments of respect—though to virtue and authority they ever made a deference; but after their plain and homely manner, yet sincere and substantial way; well remembering the example of Mordecai and Elihu; but more especially the command of their Lord and Master, Jesus Christ, who forbad his followers to call men Rabbi, which implies Lord and Master."[1] In another place, the language of the author, just quoted, is as follows: "Though we do not pull off our hats, or make courtesying, or give flattering titles, or use compliments, because we believe there is no *true* honor, but flattery and sin in the use of them; yet we treat all men with seriousness and gentleness, though it be with plainness, and our superiors with a most awful distance; and we are ready to do them any reasonable benefit or service in which we think real honor consisteth."[2] The Quaker creed then, in this particular, was to revere principles and not titles or worldly pre-eminence. They honored "all men in the Lord," but "not in the spirit and fashion of this world that passeth away." "They," truly testified the great Oliver Cromwell, "are a people whom I cannot win with gifts, honors, or places."

In conformity to the approved custom of the Society, when William Penn became a convert to Quakerism, he positively refused to take off his hat to any one. His courtly father, being exceedingly provoked at what he deemed such unreasonable conduct, tried to conciliate the youthful proselyte. He proposed a compromise, that his son should only uncover his head before three persons; to wit, the king, the duke of York, and last, but by no means least, the Admiral himself. But even this apparently innocent concession William positively declined to make. He declined to remove his hat even

---

[1] *Rise and Progress*, 32.   [2] *Select Works*, V, 26.

in the presence of his father because, as Mr. Grahame expresses it, "he refused to lay even a single grain of incense on what he deemed an unhallowed altar of human arrogance and vanity." [1]

It is related that George III, when he granted an audience to the Quakers, took care to save their honor, and at the same time spare his own royal feelings, by stationing at the door of the chamber an extra groom, whose sole duty was to remove the hats of the visitors as they approached the monarch. Such, indeed, was the obstinacy of the Friends in retaining their head gear, that one writer, in evident exasperation, declares that "their virtue lies in their hats, as Samson's did in his hair." In the archaic language of George Fox, however, it was not permissible for an individual to "bow, or scrape with his leg to any one." In the year 1705, the privilege of wearing their hats in all courts of judicature in Pennsylvania was taken away. And it was accounted an occasion of special jubilation among the inhabitants of the Colony when their invaded right was subsequently restored by Governor Keith.

The Friends even retained their hats in their religious gatherings. They did this simply because they did not regard their houses of worship more holy than any other place. The women, however, when the Spirit moved them to preach, uncovered their heads. It appears also that all hats were removed during prayers. At an early date, it had been officially decreed that "it hath seemed good to the Holy Ghost, and to us, in the performance of public prayers to the Lord, to pull off our hats." During prayers it was also customary for the audience to stand. But these were only a few of the peculiar features exhibited by their meetings for worship. The men, as a rule, sat on one side of the house; the women occupied the other. As they possessed no designated or specially ordained preacher, the absence of the pulpit desk was conspicuous. As there might be, however, several voluntary speakers, a long plat-

---

[1] *Col. Hist. of. U. S.*, I, 494.

form was erected in front of the congregation. Here sat the ministers, the men facing the males in the audience; the women, the females. Any one, who considered himself "moved thereto" had the privilege of addressing the assembly. No lines of demarcation were ever drawn between the male and female exhorters. And when the Quakers were hard pressed with the Pauline text relative to women preachers, they would naïvely reply, "Thee knows Paul was not partial to females."

In the early times, potentates, and rich men generally, were addressed in the plural; that is, as *you*, while persons belonging to the lower walks in life were almost invariably referred to as *thou*. The Society of Friends, abhorring all such artificial and invidious distinctions, condemned this custom as unchristian. They determined to address everyone alike in the singular number. Then no one could accuse them of partiality. This, as Fox assures us, was a "sore cut to proud flesh," and doubtless he spoke truly. "This, among the rest," writes William Penn, "sounded so harsh to many of them, and they took it so ill, that they would say, 'Thou *me*, thou my dog. If thou thou'st *me*, I'll thou thy teeth down thy throat,' forgetting the language *they use* to God in their own *prayers*, and the *common style* of the *Scriptures*, and that it is an *absolute* and *essential* property of speech."[1] The Quakers regarded the use of the plural number as obsequious flattery and adulation, hence their determined opposition to it. Their persistency in this matter, however, called down storms of indignant wrath and trenchant censure upon their devoted heads. A certain Mr. Jeffrey contemptuously declared, "If 'you' was applied to negroes, fellows, toad-eaters; how could the use of this pronoun be stigmatized as flattery?" He then affirms that to employ always the singular "Thou" would be just as reasonable as to talk always of our *doublets* and *hose*,

---

[1] *Select Works*, V, 223.

and eschew all mention of *coats* and *stockings* as fearful abominations.

The Quakers likewise rejected the custom of saying, good-night, good-morning, good-day, or passing the other ordinary compliments of the season. Penn excuses such behavior by alleging that "they knew the night was good and the day was good without wishing of either," hence these phrases were regarded as mere useless words, which the Friends always abhorred and endeavored to avoid. "Besides," continues Penn, "they were words and wishes of *course* and are usually as little *meant*, as are *love* and service in the custom of cap and knee; and superfluity in these, as well as in other things, was burdensome to them; and therefore they did not only decline to use them, but found themselves often pressed to reprove the practice." [1]

The members of the Society always recommended silence by example as well as by precept. They rarely employed more words than were absolutely necessary to convey the intended meaning. Penn earnestly advised his brethren and sisters in the faith to "avoid company where it is not profitable or necessary; and in those occasions, speak little; silence is wisdom, where speaking is folly." [2] Idle words and unprofitable conversation were considered as a waste of valuable time; or worse still, as inconsistent with the serious hopes, duties and responsibilities of professing Christians. The Quakers firmly believed in the wisdom of the Royal Sage, that "in all labor there is profit; but the talk of the lips tendeth only to penury." [3]

Discarding the employment of all formalism, alike in their religious services and in their private life, it is not an occasion of surprise when we discover that the Quakers rejected the practice of saying grace at the table. When their meals were served, all those assembled around the board assumed a

---

[1] *Select Works*, V, 223.
[2] *Ibid.*, V, 134.   [3] Proverbs, XIV, 23.

thoughtful attitude, with bowed heads, and maintained a rigid silence for several moments. If, during this interval no one appeared to be moved to make any utterance, they proceeded to attack the viands placed before them without additional ceremony.

The Society of Friends always entertained unmistakable aversion to games of chance—indeed, to every variety of gambling, and measures looking towards the final suppression of this iniquity were early adopted. In the Great Law of Pennsylvania, for instance, it was declared, "that if any person be Convicted of playing at Cards, Dice, Lotteries, or such like enticing, vain, and evil Sports and Games, such persons shall for every such offence, pay five shillings, or Suffer five Days Imprisonment (at hard labour) in the house of Correction."[1] But the Quakers, in their sectarian capacity, were urged to go farther. They were advised to shun even the appearance of evil, and to rigorously exclude from their possession any article that could be employed for the purposes of gambling. Despite these statutes and earnest admonitions, however, the investigator will discover that many packs of cards were annually imported into the Colony, and that too by members of the Society in high standing. In explanation of this apparent discrepancy, it will be sufficient to remark that these "devils' books" (as they were then stigmatized by individuals of pronounced religiosity) were intended for entirely different employment from that prohibited by the Colonial Legislature. Prior to the American Revolution, broadly speaking, the bits of pasteboard, which we now denominate visiting cards (by courtesy), were not known in Pennsylvania. Consequently a substitute had to be invented. And to supply this deficiency, playing cards were largely imported and extensively circulated. But they were also necessary for still other purposes. In those days their backs were entirely blank, utterly destitute of the present attempts at ornamentation, and on the spaces thus

---

[1] Linn, *Charter and Laws*, p. 144.

left vacant were imprinted invitations to receptions, tickets of admission to entertainments, and other matter of a similar character.

Other methods of diversion, which the consensus of opinion of the fashionable world agreed in regarding as innocent and even beneficial, were likewise included under the ban of Quaker displeasure. The ancient philosopher Plato constantly impressed upon the minds of his disciples the debasing character of certain kinds of music; but the good Friends, in this respect, far surpassed their illustrious prototype, for, with some trivial exceptions, they anathematized music in general, and denounced it as invariably corrupting in its tendencies. In the estimation of the founder of the Society, George Fox, such things were too redolent of the sensuous, the frivolous, the false, and the dissipated, to be admitted into the houses of professing Christians. But this aversion, apparently, was not peculiar to, or characteristic of, the Quaker sect. As early as the year 1536, the English Puritans had presented a formal protestation to their king, emphatically declaring " the playing at the organyes a foolish vanity." And the Friends, to this extent at least, following in footsteps of their dissenting brethren, strenuously opposed the introduction of musical instruments into their residences or meeting houses. Fox unhesitatingly affirms—and the majority of the inhabitants of Pennsylvania coincided perfectly in the opinion—" I was moved to cry against all kinds of music, for it burdeneth the pure life." It was "carnal wisdom to know music," and " fleshy exercise" to sing. But to prevent any misunderstanding, the erudite Barclay, in his *Truth Cleared of Calumnies*, essays to present the precise status of this most interesting question. " That singing is a part of God's worship, and is warrantably performed amongst the saints," he writes, " is a thing denied by no Quaker so called, and it is not unusual among them, and that at times David's words may be used as the Spirit leads thereunto." He proceeds, moreover, to explain that the principal objection of the Friends to the use of vocal music in their worship consisted in the fact that a "mixed multitude, known to be drunkards, swearers," &c., &c., sing, and that indifferently all descriptions of psalms and hymns. Such persons, he continues, by reason of their dissolute character, are eminently unsuitable to worship the Infinite Jehovah in this manner; and their doing so, logically argues our author, would simply "cause our worship to be a lie." From these allusions, it appears sufficiently obvious to the student of theological creeds that the singing here preferred was of a kindred nature to that indulged in by the General Baptists, which is to say, that of a single person. Thus, therefore, in the opinion of the Quakers, the saints alone might sing praise to God: concerning the wicked, the unregenerate, the Society had an abiding belief that it would be more appropriate for them to "howl for their sins."

As illustrative of their opinions concerning dancing, it will doubtless be sufficient to cite the following instance: In the year 1746, a certain Thomas Kinnett advertised to teach "the noble art of defence with small swords, and also dancing." Immediately upon the appearance of this notice, the Friends irately replied, that they were indeed "surprised at his audacity and brazen impudence in giving these *detestable vices* those high encomiums. They may be proved so far from accomplishments, that they are *diabolical.*"

Field sports also came in for their full share of condemnation at the hands of the Society, owing chiefly to the suffering they usually produced. The netting of animals for purposes of sustenance, however, was always permitted. Indeed, the killing of them in any other manner was never actually prohibited—always provided, of course, that this was done with the object of supplying food, and not for mere self-gratification.

Being strenuously opposed to bloodshed of all descriptions, sanguinary sports were extremely repugnant to the Quakers. To the Friends, the only legitimate object of hunting and fishing was "that they may be accommodated with such food and sustenance as God in His providence hath freely afforded."

To the theatre, determined opposition was made on the ground that it was a "corrupting agency." The objection appears to have rested, in addition to religious scruples, upon the supposition that it would encourage idleness, and draw large sums of money from "weak and inconsiderate persons, who are apt to be fond of such kinds of entertainments." The earliest mention, the writer has been able to discover, of a theatrical performance in the Colony of Pennsylvania occurs in January, 1749. In that year, a company composed of residents of the Province was suppressed by order of the authorities. After an interval of five years, however, an English company was licensed on the condition that their plays " be not indecent or immoral." The manager of the company was also required to devote the entire proceeds of one evening to the benefit of the indigent, and to become security for all debts or other obligations contracted by any member of his organization. The triumph of the theatre seemed to be attained in 1758, when an opera house was erected near the suburbs of Philadelphia, despite the relentless opposition of the Quakers. In the year 1759, a foreign theatrical company visited the metropolis of the Colony, and requested permission " to act their plays." The Governor allowed them to perform, under the proviso that the company should play one night for the benefit of the destitute in the Province. Most of the colonists, however, were united in their opposition to such "profane shows," and Judge Allen was nearly overwhelmed with petitions for injunctions to restrain the players. But this worthy, possibly entertaining secret fondness for such diversion himself, refused to interfere. Shortly after this circumstance, the Judge's wife suddenly died, and this domestic misfortune was regarded by many individuals as a suitable judgment upon him for affording protection to "profane stage players." The following year, that is in 1760, a law was enacted for the suppression of theatres. "Whereas," runs its phraseology, "several companies of idle persons and strollers have come into this Province from foreign parts in the characters of players, erected stages and theatres and thereon acted divers plays by which the weak, poor, and necessitous have been prevailed on to neglect their labor and industry and to give extravagant prices for their tickets and great numbers of disorderly persons have been drawn together in the night to the great distress of many poor families, manifest injury of this young Colony and grievous scandal of religion and the laws of this government. Be it therefore Enacted, That every person and persons whatsoever that from and after the First day of January which will be A. D., 1761, shall erect, build, or cause to be erected or build any play-house, theatre, stage or scaffold for acting, shewing or exhibiting any tragedy, comedy, farce, interlude, or other play, or part of a play whatsoever, or shall act, shew or exhibit them, or any of them, or be in any ways concerned therein or in selling any of the tickets aforesaid in any city, town or place within this Province, and be thereof legally convicted in manner aforesaid shall forfeit and pay the sum of five hundred pounds lawful money aforesaid."[1]

Attempts at ornamentation were also viewed with grave suspicion, because they were deemed frivolous, and anything partaking of this nature, the Quaker believed to be injurious. The houses of the Friends were generally very plain, and almost entirely innocent of any sort of adornment or ostentation. Pictures for the decoration of their dwellings were used but sparingly. Wall paper was introduced, under protest, about the year 1790. Antecedent to this date, the reign of whitewash had been universal. Carpets were at this time deemed an undesirable luxury, for fresh sand was considered more healthful. But in the march of progress they had to come, and the year 1750 is given in the books as that of their

---

[1] Seilhamer, *History of the Amer. Theatre Before The Revolution.*

advent. Sewel mentions a case where one gentleman, in his desire for simplicity, even banished from his fireside the luxury of a pair of tongs and substituted the primitive implement of a cloven stick.

The reforming hand of the Society was likewise laid on the ordinary names of the days and months. The Quakers, regarding these names as originating in mythological idolatry, discarded them as expressive of a sort of heathenish homage. Instead of these idolatrous appellations, a simple numerical nomenclature was therefore substituted. Henceforth the fourth day of the week, for example, was no longer to sport under the pagan name of Wednesday, but was to be known simply as fourth day.

The Quakers drank no healths. The Great Law of Pennsylvania expressly interdicted such "vicious" practices. The use of tobacco, in any form, was also strongly discouraged. Penn disapproved of either smoking or chewing, and he exerted himself in every possible way to terminate this "evil." A man who was discovered smoking on the street in the city of Philadelphia was fined 12 pence and admonished not to repeat the *offense*.[1] In addition to the moral, there appear to have been other important reasons, however, for this apparently arbitrary prohibition. In those early days, fire-extinguishing apparatus was in the embryonic stages of development, and conflagration constantly impended over every provincial town. Consequently the Quakers claimed that their prohibition was for the prevention of fire. In the year 1696, it had been enacted, " That no person shall presume to Smoke tobacco in the Streets, either by day or night and every person offending herein, shall forfeit for every such offense twelve

---

[1] The practice of the Friends in this particular, however, appears to have varied slightly in different localities. Thus, in North Carolina the use of "the weed" was not entirely prohibited. In 1726, all the members of the Society in this Colony were "advised to keep out of the *excess* [the italics are the writer's] of meats, drinks, and apparel, and smoking and chewing tobacco."—Hawks, *Hist. of N. C.*, II, 325.

pence, all which fines shall be paid to the respective Justices of each town, for the use of each town, and are to be employed for buying and providing Leather Buckets & other Instruments or Engines ag^t fires, for the public use of each town respectively."[1]

In the economy of the Friends, privateering, speculations, smuggling and all traffic or even the mere handling of the munitions of war, came in for their full share of disapprobation. Translating their belief into practice the good provincials never hesitated to express their strong displeasure on the occasion of any military demonstration. In 1700, when William Penn returned to Pennsylvania, some of the ardent young men, in opposition to the direct command of the magistrates, ventured to salute the Proprietor with a salvo of artillery. The operation, however, was performed in such an unscientific manner that it resulted in severe injury to several of the individuals participating. That they received little sympathy, it is superfluous to add. On the contrary the majority of the inhabitants regarded their misfortune as a providential rebuke of a tribute so unsuitable to members of their community. Instead of consolation, therefore, these aspiring youths were reminded in the language of the Scripture that "all they that take the sword, shall perish with the sword."[2]

Juridical procedure among the Friends was both curious and instructive. When the members of the Society disagreed, they seldom scolded and rarely went to law. All their disputes were adjusted by what we call, in the language of administration, Boards of Arbitration. These Peace Commissions, so to speak, arranged all difficulties arising between the Europeans and the Indians, as well as settling altercations between the Colonists themselves. As regards composition, the bodies possessing such important functions, were usually as follows:[3]

---

[1] Linn, *Charter and Laws of Prov. Pa.*, p. 260. [2] I Matt., xxvi, 52.
[3] The early Christians settled all their disputes by arbitration.—Geffcken, *Church and State*, I, 103.

Three persons were appointed by each County Court of Pennsylvania, and the individuals thus selected were invested with the honorable title of Peacemakers. Their chief duty was to mediate between contending parties, accommodating their contests, if possible, by their friendly services. Appeal to the usual course of the law was, however, permitted when one party refused to refer the matter in question to the Peacemakers, or when the point at issue could only be settled by the ordinary legal proceedings. When a Friend disagreed with a person outside the pale of the Society, he first proposed arbitration; if this proposition was rejected, he then had no scruples about having recourse to the courts. Some of their disputes were very easily adjusted. In 1684, for instance, we read that "there being a Difference depending between" Andrew Johnson and Hance Peterson, "the Govr & Councill advised them to shake hands, and to forgive One another; and Ordered that they should Enter in Bonds for fifty pounds apiece, for their good abearance, wch accordingly they did."[1]

Agesilaus, the famous King of Sparta, being asked on one occasion, "what ought children to learn?" quickly responded, "that which they ought to practice when they become men." With this opinion, Penn's belief coincided exactly. At an early period in his administration of the Quaker Colony he ordered that "all children within this province of the age of twelve years, shall be taught some useful trade or skill to the end none may be idle, but the poor may work to live, and the rich, if they become poor, may not want." He explains that his reason for this legislation was, that the children of the wealthy classes in England " were too generally brought up in pride and sloth, good for nothing to themselves or others." He took special care, therefore, that ample provision for the education of the young should be made in Pennsylvania. In his Frame of Government, Penn declared that a committee on manners, education, and art, should be appointed, so that

---

[1] *Col. Rec. of Pa.*, I, 52.

all "wicked and scandalous living may be prevented, and that youth may be trained up in virtue, and useful arts and knowledge." As early as 1683, an educational institution was established for the instruction of the children of the colonists. In that year " the Govr and Prov^{ll} Councill having taken into their Serious Consideration the great Necessity there is of a School Master for ye Instruction & Sober Education of Youth in the towne of Philadelphia, Sent for Enoch Flower, an Inhabitant of the said Towne, who for twenty year past hath been Exercised in that care and Imploym^t in England, to whom having Communicated their Minds, he embraced it upon these following Termes: to Learn to read English 4^s by the Quarter, to Learn to read and write 6^s by ye Quarter, to learn to read, Write and Cast acc^t 8^s by ye Quarter; for Boarding a Scholler, that is to say, dyet, Washing, Lodging, & Schooling, Tenn pounds for one whole year."[1]

In 1689, the Quakers opened another school for "all children and servants, male and female—the rich, at reasonable rates; the poor, for nothing." George Keith was made principal of this foundation, and was assisted by a certain Thomas Makin, who, the records inform the reader, was "a good Latinist." The plan of instruction was similar to that of an ordinary modern grammar school, with the exception that its curriculum included " the learned languages." It was entirely supported by the Friends, but representatives of all denominations were magnanimously permitted to share its advantages. In the year 1749, Franklin published his " Proposal Relative to the Education of Youth in Pennsylvania," which resulted in the establishment of the Academy. This institution was promoted to collegiate rank about 1755; and, finally, in 1779, it was incorporated as the University of Pennsylvania.[2]

---

[1] *Col. Rec. of Pa.*, I, 36.
[2] In addition to the branches usually included in the curricula of such institutions, Chapter LX, of the Great Law of Pennsylvania, was particular to specify "That the Laws of this Province, from time to time, shall be

In the early days of the Colony, great care was exercised to secure competent teachers. To this end, no person was permitted to "keep school" without first securing a license, and this document could only be obtained by satisfactorily passing the requisite examination. In 1693, Thomas Meakin (our former acquaintance, now the victim of paronomasia) "keeper of the ffree schoole in the town of Philadelphia, being called before the Lt. Go^r and Councill, was told that hee must not keepe school without a License, ansred that hee was willing to comply, and to take a Licence; was therefore ordered to procure a Certificate of his abilitie, Learning & diligence, from the Inhabitants of note in this towne . . . in order to the obtaining of a Licence, which he promised to do."[1]

Notwithstanding the fact that so much attention was lavished on education in general, the age preceding the Declaration of Independence was not very favorable to the growth and development of the press and journalism. Only three papers were published in Philadelphia anterior to the American Revolution. These were *The American Weekly Mercury, The Pennsylvania Journal and Weekly Advertiser,* and *The Pennsylvania Gazette.* In 1719, the earliest venture was made. In that year, *The Mercury* first appeared. Its existence, however, was always extremely precarious, and in 1746, the paper was finally discontinued. Four years prior to this event, another paper had celebrated its *debut* in the Colony. This was *The Pennsylvania Journal and Weekly Advertiser.* Its dimensions were insignificant, corresponding to a sheet of ordinary foolscap paper. Franklin had commenced the publication of his paper, *The Gazette,* as early as 1729, and it maintained an independent existence until the middle of the

---

published and printed, that every person may have the knowledge thereof; and they shall be one of the Books taught in the Schools of this Province and territorys thereof." In the light of this provision, no one could truthfully plead ignorance of the law as an excuse.

[1] *Col. Rec. of Pa.,* Vol. I, p. 345.

succeeding century, when this publication was merged with another periodical.

There are certain constant factors in almost every community —namely, marriage and giving in marriage. Cupid exhibited as much activity in the Quaker Colony as he did in other portions of the terrestrial globe. At the time, however, of which we write, bashfulness and modesty in youth were regarded as ornaments, nay even as great virtues. "Young lovers," says Watson, "then listened and took side-long glances when before their parents or elders."[1] But, how these hopefuls behaved in the absence of the aforesaid worthies, we are not informed, for the annalist breaks off suddenly at this point, as if fearful of startling dénouements if the narrative were further continued.

Marriage among the Friends was a very important institution, and weddings were always the occasions of great festivity. The matches appear to have arisen solely from inclination. "Never marry but for love," is William Penn's advice to all, "but see that thou lovest what is lovely."[2] The Quakers, moreover, gave considerable publicity to the celebration of marriage. Before the union could be consummated, the intentions of the persons concerned were promulgated by affixing a declaration to that effect on the Court or Meetinghouse door; and when the act was finally solemnized at least twelve subscribing witnesses had to be present.

In regard to the ceremony employed, it will be sufficient to remark that they rejected the mode adopted by the Protestant sects, as well as that employed by the Roman Catholic Church, and introduced a simple form of marriage in the meeting of their own Society. The priest and the ring were discarded as being utterly heathenish. "Ceremonies," declares Penn, "they have refused not out of humor, but conscience reasonably grounded; inasmuch as no Scripture-example tells us, that the priest had any other part, of old time, than that of a

---

[1] *Annals*, I, 174.   [2] *Select Works*, V, 129.

witness among the rest, before whom the Jews used to take one another; and therefore this people look upon it as an imposition, to advance the power and profits of the clergy; and for the use of the ring, it is enough to say, that it was an heathenish and vain custom, and never practiced among the people of God, *Jews* or *primitive Christians.*"[1]

The Friends, in the language of George Fox, declared, "We marry none, but are witnesses of it; marriage being God's joining, not man's." Penn said the Quakers believed "that marriage is an ordinance of God, and that God only can rightly join men and women in marriage."[2] When a marriage was contemplated, the Monthly Meeting had to be notified of it, and the form of the paper submitted to this assembly was about as follows: "We, the subscribers, A. B., son of C., and D. B.; and F. G., daughter of H., and I. G., purpose taking each other in marriage, which we hereby offer for the approbation of Friends." Then followed the signatures of the contracting individuals. If no sufficient reasons were discovered for preventing the union, the hymeneal ceremony was performed at the appointed time.

Originally, the weddings even of the unostentatious members of the Society were very expensive and the ceremonies harrassing to the wedded—in fact, to all but the invited guests. The company usually assembled early in the morning, remained to dinner, possibly even to supper. For two entire days, it was customary to deal out refreshments with a lavish hand to all who honored the family with their presence. The gentlemen congratulated the groom on the first floor of the dwelling, and then ascended to the second story, where they wished future felicity to the blushing bride. After these preliminaries, this unfortunate female was compelled, by the unwritten law of the time, to undergo the ordeal of being kissed by all the male visitors.

---

[1] *Select Works*, V, 225. [2] *Rise and Progress*, 35.

It is somewhat astonishing, when we reflect, that the Quakers, strenuously opposed, as they unquestionably were, to all sorts of frivolity and ceremony, ever submitted to such veritable nuisances as these weddings soon turned out to be. The annalist, Watson, relates on credible authority, that it was nothing uncommon for families in affluent circumstances to have "120 persons to dine—the same who had signed their certificate of marriage at the Monthly Meeting." "These," he adds, "also partook of tea and supper."[1] At first, these elaborate ceremonies were accepted, if not without question, certainly without expressed opposition. Finally, however, the good Friends revolted from all this worldly excitement and round of festivity. At length, such frivolities were relegated to the limbo of exploded vanities, and matrimonial alliances were attended with no other ceremony than that of the parties taking each other by the hand in public meeting and avowing their willingness to enter the connubial state. After these informal exercises, the marriage certificate was registered in the record book belonging to the Meeting where the marriage was solemnized, and this simple act completed the ceremony.

If the union were blessed with issue, all ceremony was likewise rejected in naming the offspring. As a rule, children were named by their parents in the presence of a mid-wife, or of those that were present at the birth. These witnesses subsequently affixed their signatures to the natal certificate, and this paper was then duly recorded in the book of that Monthly Meeting to which the parents belonged.

The funeral customs of the Friends were as unostentatious as their form of marriage. The body of the deceased was generally taken to the nearest meeting-house so as to accommodate relatives and acquaintances, who might desire to attend the interment. Here a short pause was made, during which any person, who felt himself moved to speak, was at liberty

---

[1] *Annals*, I, 178.

to address the assembled congregation. The corpse was then conveyed to the cemetery, usually by several young men. When the burial ground was reached, the pall bearers deposited the body so that the relatives might take their last look at the remains of their departed loved one. This procedure was moreover to the end that "the spectators have a sense of mortality, by the occasion then given them to reflect upon their own latter end."[1] Thomas Story, who was present at the funeral of William Penn, describes his experience in the following words: "A solid time of worship we had together, but few words among us for some time. . . . I accompanied the corpse to the grave, where we had a large meeting."

No mourning was ever worn for departed friends. Crape was accounted as especially heathenish, and not in accordance with Biblical precepts. Penn declares "that what mourning is fit for a Christian to have, at the departure of a beloved relation or friend should be worn in the mind, which is only sensible of the loss."[2] Even the casket was denied its usual black covering.[3]

No vaults were used. Tombstones were also rejected. They were considered an especial abomination. In a word, the Friends dispensed with all kinds of ceremonies. The Society regarded the substance of things; not mere external appearances.

The Quakers, in all transactions with their fellow men, endeavored to preserve the strictest honesty, and in some instances, the reader with difficulty represses a smile at the form this integrity assumed. In 1721, for example, we find the curious statement that a certain William Ganlan was fined "as he did with his breath and wind blow up the meat of his calf, whereby the meat was made unwholesome to the human body." Another case occurred in the year 1700. "Upon

---

[1] Penn, *Select Works*, V, 226.   [2] *Ibid.*
[3] "The corpse being in a *plain coffin*, without any *covering* or *furniture* upon it.—*Penn's Works*, V, 226.

Complaint of ye poor ag^t ye bakers of bread for sale not being of the Law^{11} & due assize," so runs the language of the record, "Justinian Fox, Jno Sawtell, Aurther Holton, Wm. Royal, Geo. Abbiott, Marie Merryweather, Tho. Hall & Hugh Derburrow, being summoned appeared to whom the Go^v notified ye said Complaint; Who generallie ansred, y^t tho it was hard for you to Live by itt, wheat being now 5s. 6d. p. bush., & y^t they buing but smal stocks wer outt-bid by the eminent merts and bolters; yet hoped y^r bread was of ye due assize, the prov. & Go^v advised you to be conformable to ye Laws in that behalfe made, & said hee would appoint a Clark of ye market to ye end."[1]

Dentistry appears to have found no very congenial soil in early Pennsylvania. Tooth brushes were an unheard-of luxury; an innovation not to be tolerated even in thought. The most fastidious and respectable individuals were content to rub their teeth with a chalked rag, or, worse still, with snuff; while some conservative persons even went so far as to deem it an unmistakable token of effeminacy in men to be caught cleaning their teeth at all. At this period, the dental art had scarcely emerged from its rude beginnings. But, curiously enough, some of the triumphs of which the present century is so proud, were well known at this time. Reference is especially made to the process of *transplanting* teeth, as it was then called. By a printed advertisement, which appeared in the year 1784, Dr. Le Mayeur, one of the first dentists who practiced in the city of Philadelphia, engaged to pay two guineas for each tooth which may be offered him by "persons disposed to sell their front teeth, or any of them." These were wanted for the operation, technically denominated *transplanting*, by which a perfect tooth is extracted from the mouth of one living person and embedded in that of another. This enterprising doctor appears to have been extremely successful in his specialty, for it is authentically

---

[1] *Col. Rec. of Pa.*, I, 546.

related that he "transplanted" as many as 123 teeth in the comparatively short space of six months.[1]

The field of employment in colonial Pennsylvania was well-nigh unlimited, and scarcity of work was a thing unheard of. The industrious could always find congenial employment without much difficulty. The hours of labor as well as the times for refreshment appear to have been regulated in the various trades, and were generally announced by the ringing of bells.

In some respects, the Philadelphia of this period reminds the historical student of Geneva at the time of Calvin. After nine o'clock at night, the officers—at first all private citizens serving in succession—inspected the town, and no inhabitant thereof was permitted to remain at any ordinary[2] after that hour without good and sufficient reason. "It is worthy of commendation," writes Thomas Chakeley, in his interesting journal, "that our Governor, Thomas Lloyd, sometimes in the evening, before he went to rest, used to go in person to the public houses, and order the people he found there to their own houses, till at length he was instrumental to promote the better order, and did in a great measure suppress vice and immorality in the city" of Philadelphia.

Originally, the Quakers prescribed no particular style of dress; for, in their judgment, it was "no vanity to use what the country naturally produced," and they reproved nothing but that extravagance in raiment which "all sober men of all sorts readily grant to be evil." Wigs were at this period à la mode, and even the inhabitants of Pennsylvania succumbed to the seductive influences of this worldly custom. In the year 1719, a prominent Friend, ordering his wearing apparel, writes, "I want for myself and my three sons, each a wig— light, gud bobs." Even Franklin, disdainful as he was of display and artificiality, wore a tremendous horse-hair wig.

---

[1] *U. S. Census* (1880) *Social. Stat. of Cities*, I, 785.
[2] The ancient word for inn or hotel.

And Penn's private expense book reveals the startling fact that even the Proprietary of the Province indulged in these vanities to the extent of four wigs per annum.

In early times, too, the Quaker women wore their colored silk aprons as did the aristocratic ladies of other denominations. And the wealthy female members of the Society also arrayed themselves in white satin petticoats embroidered with flowers, and pearl satin gowns, with peach-colored cloaks of the same material. Their white and shapely necks were ornamented with delicate lawn or lace, and also with charms. In course of time, however, white aprons were discarded by the *élite*, and then the Friends abandoned colors and adopted white. The Quaker ladies also wore immense beaver hats, which had scarcely any crown, and were fastened to the head by silken cords tied in a bewitching bow under the chin. This was the so-called *Skimming dish* hat. Such a bonnet was purchased for seven or eight dollars, when beaver fur was plentiful. To be sure, even this was a somewhat extravagant price, but with the exercise of proper care such a hat was a life-long investment. If it were not a thing of beauty, yet it might be a joy forever.

The Quaker dress, however, gradually assumed a more subdued form. Subsequently, broad-brimmed hats, coats with straight collars, the peculiar female dress—articles so familiar in our own day—were introduced. Drab eventually became the prevailing color for the ladies. Metallic buttons, so fashionable at this time, were not used by the Friends. When shoe buckles were worn with so much display, the good Quakers employed leather straps as answering the purpose equally well, and being more consistent with their profession as disciples and followers of the lowly Nazarene. Thus the wearing apparel became more and more simplified until Penn unhesitatingly declares, "if thou art clean and warm it is sufficient; for more clothes but robs the poor, and pleases the wanton."[1]

---

[1] *Select Works*, V, 128.

In the year 1771, the first umbrellas made their appearance in Philadelphia, and were scouted by the more conservative as ridiculous affectations. Afterwards, however, when the important character of their services was more fully understood and appreciated, their reception was decidedly more cordial.

In Quaker theology, all magic and exorcism were relegated to their own place, to the world of phantoms. While other colonies were fairly intoxicated with sorcery; when the theory of witches' marks was conscientiously believed in as an appendix to Revelation; when the spitting of pins by the plaintiff demonstrated beyond all peradventure diabolical influences, and was regarded as sufficient evidence to send the unfortunate defendant to the gallows; when decrepit old women were supposed to find indescribable delight in cantering through space on the conventional broomstick, and in performing other gymnastics, as unknown to common sense as to reason—while all this was believed elsewhere, we discover only one such case in the Province of Pennsylvania. This occurred on the 27th day of December, in the year 1683, when one Margaret Mattson was indicted and tried on the charge of being a confirmed witch. The accusation against her consisted of a number of vague, incoherent, and irrational stories. It was related of her that she bewitched calves, geese, and had caused unsuspecting cows to do many queer and truly thaumaturgic acts. A certain "Henry Drystreet attested, Saith he was tould 20 years agoe, that the prisoner at the Barr was a Witch, & that severall Cows were bewitched by her; also that James Saunderling's mother tould him that she bewitched her Cow, but afterwards said it was a mistake, and that her Cow should doe well againe, for it was not her Cow, but an Other Person's that should dye." Moreover, even Mrs. Mattson's daughter testified to the astounding fact that her mother was beyond all question in league with his satanic majesty. Notwithstanding, however, all this weight of testimony, the jury, after receiving the charge from the judge brought in the rather ambiguous verdict that they found her "Guilty of having the Common fame of a Witch, but not Guilty in manner and form as Shee Stands Indicted."[1] Conviction would have been almost pardonable in a day when men like Richard Baxter and Cotton Mather did not hesitate to record their faith in "a God, a devil, and witchcraft"—at a time when John Wesley positively declared that to give up witchcraft would be to surrender the Bible itself, and when even the great Quaker, George Fox, believed in "familiar spirits." William Penn, however, incorporated no such fatuous doctrine among his accepted beliefs, and the alleged witch was accordingly released. By this judicious conduct, Pennsylvania, in all probability, escaped the odium of Salem.

On one occasion, Coleridge described a Quaker as "a curious combination of ice and flame," signifying thereby that he was essentially an extremist. With all possible deference to the opinion of the English poet, it must be said, however, that one may ransack history in vain for substantiation and verification of this assertion. Examination invariably discovers the Friends ranging themselves on the side of moderation. No one, who candidly and impartially investigates their customs, can escape this conclusion, even were he so inclined. Feasts, fastings—excesses, in general, received their most unqualified condemnation, and that from the earliest dawn of their history down to the present generation. Like a steamship attempting to enter some rock-bound harbor, like that of St. John's, in the Island of New Foundland, the Society believed that only by avoiding extremes, the perilous headlands on either side of the entrance, could they reasonably expect to find a channel that would conduct them past dangerous obstructions into the tranquil haven beyond.

---

[1] *Col. Recs. of Pa.*, I, 40–41.

II.

QUAKER LEGISLATION.

In the language of what might be designated as the Constitution of Pennsylvania, it was announced that the governmental machinery of the Colony was to consist of the Governor and freemen of the said province, in form of a Provincial Council and General Assembly, "and further that these two political bodies, by and with the consent of the Governor aforesaid, should pass all the necessary enactments, select and appoint all public functionaries—in short, transact official business of every sort."[1]

In composition, however, neither the Council nor the Assembly offers any essential characteristics that distinguish them from the corresponding legislative bodies existing in the other colonies. The freemen were simply empowered to select "out of themselves seventy-two persons of most note for their wisdom, virtue, and ability," who were to be "called and act as the Provincial Council of the said Province."[2] One-third of the members constituting this body were to retire annually. Moreover "in this Provincial Council, the Governor or his deputy shall or may always preside, and have a treble voice; and the said Provincial Council shall always continue, and sit upon its own adjournments and committees."[3] It was farther provided that not less than two-thirds of the whole Council was to constitute a quorum. And "to the end that all laws prepared by the Governor and Provincial Council aforesaid, may yet have the more full concurrence of the free-

---

[1] *Frame*, Sec. I.   [2] *Ibid.*, Sec. II.   [3] *Ibid.*, Sec. VI.

men of the province, it is declared, granted, and confirmed, that at the time and place or places for the choice of a Provincial Council as aforesaid, the said freedmen shall yearly choose members to serve in General Assembly as their representatives, not exceeding two hundred persons."[1] And provision was also made that all elections were to be by ballot.

In this Frame, it was likewise stated "that for the better establishment of the Government and laws of this province, and to the end there may be an universal satisfaction in the laying of the fundamentals thereof; the General Assembly shall or may for the first year consist of all the freemen of and in said province, and ever after it shall be yearly chosen as aforesaid; which number of two hundred shall be enlarged as the country shall increase in people, so as it do not exceed five hundred at any time."[2] But even the number two hundred was never reached. It was soon ascertained to be inconvenient, and was therefore abandoned. The first Assembly only contained seventy-two members, and its successors were usually composed of thirty-six persons, distributed among the different counties and the city of Philadelphia.

In the year 1696, the system of representation was somewhat modified. Then it was determined that "two persons out of each of the Counties of this government" were "to serve as the peoples' Representatives in Council;" and that "four persons out of each of the said Counties" were "to serve as Representatives in Assembly."[3] No law could be proposed in the more popular branch, except such as had been previously considered by the Governor and his Council. This provision almost carries the mind back to Athenian politics, where the same precaution was ascertained to be necessary. In spite of the fact, however, that the Assembly could not originate legislation, it possessed many important functions. That astute statesman, Frederick the Great of Prussia, once declared that "Finance was the pulse of the State." As the Assembly

---

[1] *Ibid.*, Sec. XIV.   [2] Sec. XVI.   [3] *Frame of* 1696, Sec. II.

controlled the purse strings of the Colony, it was virtually invested with the political supremacy.

Such then, in outline, was the governing body of Pennsylvania. The first General Assembly of the Province was convened at Chester in 1682, at which time the Great Law was passed. The first formal, political body that ever assembled in the city of Philadelphia was held at the Friends' meetinghouse the succeeding year, that is, in 1683. The Government was now completely organized. It speedily commenced to busy itself in legislation, and as many of its chief peculiarities are to be sought in activity of this description, we may glance at some of the more striking and characteristic enactments.

The one notable measure passed by the first Assembly of Philadelphia was that referring disputes to arbitration. The law provided that three *peacemakers*, after the manner of common arbitrators, were to be selected by each county court, that they might hear and terminate all controversies and differences.[1] Some very amusing sumptuary laws were also introduced during this session. For instance, it was proposed that no inhabitant should be permitted to have more than two suits of wearing apparel; one ostensibly intended for summer; the other for winter. Other members, possibly proceeding upon the principle that misery loves company, advocated the measure that young men be compelled to enter into matrimonial alliances upon the acquisition of a specified age. But the majority of the Quakers were not prepared for such drastic enactments as these; consequently, the propositions in question were dropped.

Other more important matters demanded attention. All through their history, the Quakers strenuously opposed all unlawful sensual indulgences; consequently the authorities

---

[1] In 1683, a "Petition of Rich'd Wells" was read, and "Ordered that he be referred to ye Peacemakers, and in case of Refusal to ye County Court, according to Law." *Col. Rec. of Pa.*, Vol. I, p. 34.

soon began to legislate for the suppression of irregularities of this description. It was, indeed, the very first Assembly convened in the metropolis (if the expression be allowed) which enacted the following law:[1] "And to prevent Clandestine, Loose, and unseemly proceedings in this Province and territories thereof, about marriage, *Be it*, &c., That all marriages not forbidden by the law of God, shall be encouraged; But the parents and guardians shall be, if possible, first Consulted; And the parties clearnes from all other engagements assured by a Certificate from some Crediable persons where they had lived; And by their affixing of their intentions of Marriage on the Court or Meeting-house Door of the County wherein they Dwell, one Month before the solemnizing thereof; And their said Marriage shall be solemnized by taking one another as husband and wife, before Sufficient Witnesses; And a certificate of the whole under the hands of parties and witnesses (at least twelve) shall be brought to the Register of the County, where they are Marryed, and be Registered in his office. And if any person shall presume to marry or to join any in Marriage Contrary hereunto, such person so Marrying shall pay ten pounds, and such person so joining others in Marriage shall pay twenty pounds."[2]

By the authority of the Great Law of Pennsylvania, it was declared that "no person, be it either widower or widow, shall contract marriage, much less marry, under one year after the

---

[1] *Ibid.*, p. 151. Re-enacted in 1690, and again in 1693.
[2] November 20, 1703, the President made complaint "agst Andrew Bankson, one of ye Justices of Philada County, for irregularly marrying a couple lately according to law, but against ye Prohibitions of ye Parents." When brought before the Council the Justice "declared that he was wholly ignorant of its being illegal, & was heartily sorry for what was done, promising that whether he should continue in Commission, or otherwise, this should be such a caution to him as to prevent him of committing the like for ye future, & being severely checked, was dismissed." *Col. Rec. of Pa.*, II, 115.

3

decease of his wife or her husband."¹ In 1690, it was enacted that any one committing adultery should² "for the first offense be publicly whipt and suffer one whole year's imprisonment in the house of Correction at hard labour, to the behoof of the publick." For a second infraction of the law, the penalty was "imprisonment in manner aforesaid During Life."³

Incest and bigamy, being transgressions of a similar character, were likewise severely punished. In 1705, the punishment of these offences was somewhat modified. In order that imprisonment provided for by the penal law might be dreaded, in 1682 a bill had been passed to the effect that "all prisons will be work-houses for felons, Thiefs, Vagrants, and Loose, abusive and Idle persons whereof one shall be in every county."⁴

Next to impurity in point of heinousness to the Quakers, came profanity,⁵ and at an early date measures were adopted for its suppression. In 1682, the organic law of the Colony upon this subject was, "That whosoever Shall Swear in their Common Conversation, by the name of God, or Christ, or Jesus, being Legally Convicted thereof, shall pay for every such offence five shillings, or suffer five days' imprisonment in the house of Correction, at hard labour, to the behoof of the publick, and be fed with bread and water only, During that

---

¹ This regulation as regards the females is found in the ancient Saxon law, which prohibited a widow from intermarrying within twelve months after the decease of her consort. Vide Ll. Ethel, A. D., 1008. Ll. Canut, c. 71. The purpose of this provision was to establish, with certainty, the paternity of the progeny. If the widow were permitted to enter into new matrimonial alliances, within the ordinary period of gestation, after the determination of the coverture, the issue would have two putative fathers, thus making the real parent impossible of ascertainment. Trivial as this matter may appear to the uninitiated layman, those acquainted with the laws of inheritance need not be reminded that the subject is one of considerable importance.

² Constantine made adultery a capital crime.   ³ Linn, 194.

⁴ *Great Law of Pa.* Chap. LIX. Re-enacted in 1690.

⁵ *Great Law of Pa.*, Chap. LIV. Re-enacted in 1690.

time. . . . Whosoever Shall Swear by any other thing or name, and is Legally convicted thereof, shall for every such offence, pay half a Crown or suffer three days' imprisonment in the house of Correction, at hard labour, having only bread and water for their sustenance."[1]

This law was substantially re-enacted in 1690.[2] It was then declared " that whosoever shall, in their Conversation at any time curse himself or another or any other thing belonging to himself or any other, and is Legally convicted thereof, Shall pay for every such offence five shillings, or suffer five days' imprisonment as aforesaid."[3] Speaking obscenely was also punishable by a fine.

In the year 1700, legislative activity produced a new law against cursing. An act was then introduced and approved " to prevent the grievous Sins of cursing and Swearing within this Province and Territories." The wording of the statute was as follows: " Be it Further Enacted by the Authority aforesaid, That whosoever shall willfully, premeditatedly and despitefully, blaspheme or speak loosely and profanely of Almighty God, Christ Jesus, the Holy Spirit, or the Scriptures of Truth, and is legally convicted thereof, shall forfeit and pay the sum of *Ten Pounds*, for the Use of the Poor of the County, where such offence shall be committed, or suffer three months' Imprisonment at hard Labour as aforesaid, for the Use of the said Poor."[4] From the records we glean that a butcher was indicted in 1702 as a common swearer " for swearing three oaths in the market place, and for uttering two very bad curses."[5] Although this language can scarcely fail to

---

[1] *Ibid.*, Chaps. III and IV.
[2] And again in 1697.
[3] Linn, 193.
[4] *Laws of Pa.*, Vol. I, p. 6.
[5] In 1690, President Lloyd, on the basis of a letter received from "a very Credible person," endeavored to exclude Thomas Clifton from the Council, alleging "that he was not for Yea and Nay, but for God Damm You." The charge was denied by the said Clifton, and the Board " having only paper Evidence, Resolved that He be admitted at present, but upon further proof made of ye ffact, Immediately dismissed." *Col. Rec. of Pa.*, I, 282.

provoke a smile on the part of the reader, it bears sufficient evidence to the fact that the Quakers did not intend their laws to be mere ornaments on their statute books. Even the best intentioned human efforts, however, are not always successful, and notwithstanding the earnest endeavors of the Friends to the contrary, the "cursing and swearing" did not completely disappear. Even as late as 1746, we discover that still another measure was approved, entitled "An Act for the more effectual suppression of profane cursing and swearing."[1]

Any one in Pennsylvania who was rash enough to offer, or to accept a challenge to fight a duel paid dearly for the luxury. The law of 1682 took especial care to provide " that whosoever shall Challenge another person to fight, hee that Challengeth and hee that accepted the Challenge, shall for every such offence, pay five pounds, or suffer three months' imprisonment in the House of Correction at hard Labour."[2] A similar enactment was passed in 1690, and this was followed by an act adopted ten years later, " to prevent all Duelling and fighting of Duells within this Province and Territories."[3]

In supposed harmony with the regulations of the Scriptures, capital offences were punished by execution. In 1683, the law was framed and passed providing "that if any person within this Province, or territories thereof, Shall wilfully or premeditately kill another person, or wilfully or premeditately be the cause of, or accessory to the Death of any person, Such person Shall, according to the law of God, Suffer Death: And one half of his Estate shall go to his wife and Children; And if no Wife nor Children, then to the next of his kindred, not Descending Lower than the third Degree; to be Claimed within three years after his Death; And the other half of his estate to be Disposed of, as the Governor shall see meet."[4]

But other transgressions were not forgotten, especially was this true of the "unruly member." As early as 1683, a law

---

[1] *Ibid.*, Vol. I, p. 212.
[3] *Laws of Pa.*, Vol. I, p. 6.
[2] *Great Law of Pa.* See XXV.
[4] Linn, p. 144. Re-enacted in 1690.

had passed the Assembly " to the end that the Exorbitancy of the tongue may be bridled and Rebuked, *Be it* &c., That every person Convicted before any Court or Magistrate for Rallying or Scolding; Shall Stand one whole hour in the most public place, where Such offence was Committed, with a Gagg in their Mouth or pay five shillings."[1] In 1701, the Assembly passed another law for the punishment of the "vices of Scolding, drunkenness, and for the restraining of the practice drinking healths." Drunkenness was always regarded by the Quakers as a sin of considerable enormity, consequently they put forth their utmost endeavors for the suppression of this iniquity. It had been enacted in the year 1682, that any person found "abusing himself with Drink unto Drunkenness was, for the first offence to pay five shillings, or work five days in the house of Correction at hard Labour and be fed only with bread and water; and for the second offence, and ever after, ten shillings, or ten days labour as aforesaid." And those "who doe suffer such excess of Drinking att their houses, shall be liable to the same punishment with the Drunkard."[2] In 1683, we ascertain that a certain John Richardson was compelled to pay "five shillings for being disordered in Drink," and that he was sharply rebuked for his wickedness."[3] But this example it appears did not deter Timothy Metcalf from indulging in similar dissipation, for the record avers that he was guilty of unseemly conduct owing to his looking on the wine when it was red.

Gambling was always specially hateful to the Quakers, and measures were early employed for its prevention. Indeed the Great Law of Pennsylvania itself declared, "That if any person be Convicted of playing at Cards, Dice, Lotteries, or such like enticing, vain, and evil Sports and Games, such persons shall, for every such offence, pay five shillings, or Suffer five

---

[1] *Ibid.*, p. 145.
[2] *Great Law of Pa.*, Chaps. XII–XIII. Re-enacted in 1690.
[3] *Col. Rec.*, I, 4.

Days Imprisonment (at hard labour) in the house of Correction."¹

Along with the immigrants belonging to the Society, a great many persons had "filtered" into the Colony who had very little regard for religion in general and the Christian Sabbath in particular. For the benefit of such individuals, the Assembly was careful to pass a law in the year 1690. "That Looseness, Irreligion, and Atheism," it reads, "may not creep in under the pretence of Conscience in this Province, *Be it further Enacted by the authority aforesaid*, That, according to the example of the primitive Christians, and for the ease of the Creation, Every first day of the week, called the Lord's Day, People shall abstain from their usual and common toil and labour, That whether Masters, Parents, Children, or Servants, they may the better dispose themselves to read the Scriptures of truth at home, or frequent such meetings of Religious worship abroad, as may best sute their respective persuasions."² Such was the measure of 1690. It was substantially re-enacted in the year 1705, when a statute was passed entitled, "An act to restrain People from Labour on the First day of the Week." It went on to state that "according to the Example of the primitive Christians, and for the Ease of the Creation, every First Day of the Week, commonly called *Sunday*, all People shall abstain from Toil and Labour, that whether Masters, Parents, Children, Servants, or others, they may the better dispose themselves to read and hear the Holy Scriptures of Truth at Home, and frequent such Meetings of religious Worship Abroad, as may best suit their respective Persuasions." Nothing in this enactment, however, was to "prevent the Victualling-houses, or other public House or Place from supplying the necessary Occasions of Travellers, Inmates, Lodgers, or others, on the First Day of the Week with. Victuals and Drink *in moderation*, for Reefreshment." Then follows the curious clause, "of which

---

[1] Chap. XXVII.   [2] Linn, p. 192.

necessary Occasion for Refreshment, as also Moderation, the Magistrate before whom Complaint is made shall be Judge, any Law, Usage or Custom, in this Province to the contrary notwithstanding."[1]

Thus it will be observed that the good Quakers, in their zeal and anxiety for the spiritual welfare of humanity, did not entirely ignore the more material side of the question, to wit—the temporal requirements of man. Yet, in strict accordance with the customs of the Society, the refreshment administered was always to be *in moderation*. If these bounds were passed, the person was regarded as a transgressor, and as such was subject to the prescribed penalty. Violations of the Sunday Laws were generally punished by the imposition of fines. For instance, laboring on the Sabbath incurred a forfeiture of 20 shillings; while tippling in a tavern on that day could only be atoned for by a fine of 10 shillings. It is a noteworthy fact that there was not so much Sabbatarian legislation in Pennsylvania as we find burdening the statute books of Virginia, Massachusetts, and some of the other colonies, and yet the sacredness of the day was rigidly enforced—with what strictness even a cursory perusal of the records will acquaint the investigator. In 1703, for example, we find that a certain barber was presented to the grand jury for "trimmings on the first day of the week."

In the Quaker economy, the obedience of children to their parents was always emphasized, was, in truth, enforced by law. The act, which passed in 1690, stipulated that any one assaulting his or her parent was to be "committed to the house of Correction, and there remain at hard labour, during the pleasure of the said parent."[2]

The Friends opposed the so-called *heathenish* names of the days and months. If the world persisted in clinging to this "barbarous" custom, the Society determined it would not. A law regulating the matter was therefore introduced in the

---

[1] *Laws of Pa.*, Vol. I, pp. 24–5.   [2] Linn, p. 196.

year 1682. Its phraseology runs as follows: "That the Days of the week, and Months of the year, shall be called as in Scripture, and not by heathen names (as are vulgarly used), as the First, Second, and Third days of the week; and beginning with the day called Sunday, and the month called March."[1]

Religious freedom meant a great deal to the Quaker. He had only obtained ecclesiastical liberty after passing through severe persecution, but now that he possessed it, he determined that others should share this inestimable privilege with him. To the end that this sentiment might be incorporated into the organic law of the Colony, an act was passed in the year 1690, which declared that "no person, now, or at any time hereafter, Living in this Province, who shall confess and acknowledge one Almighty God to be the Creator, Upholder and Ruler of the world, And who professes, him, or herself Obliged in Conscience to Live peaceably and quietly under the civil Government, shall in any case be molested or prejudiced for his, or her conscientious persuaion or practice, nor shall hee or shee at any time be compelled to frequent or Maintain anie religious worship, place or Ministry whatsoever Contrary to his, or her mind, but shall freely and fully enjoy his, or her, Christian Liberty in that respect, without any Interruption or reflexion. And if any person shall abuse or deride any other, for his, or her, different persuasion and practice in matters of religion, such person shall be lookt upon as a Disturber of the peace, and be punished accordingly."[2]

The liberality of the Quaker government comes out clearly also in an enactment that was passed in 1710. In that year, the Assembly gave its assent to a measure to the effect that "every one of whatever religious views he might be, who could not conscientiously make an Oath in the form and manner that was done in Britain, should have liberty to make his affirmation in the Quaker manner, that is to say, when any

---

[1] *Great Law of Pa.*, Chap. XXXV.   [2] Linn, p. 192.

one is by law called upon to assume any office or testify in any matter, that that shall not be demanded as in the presence of Almighty God, according to the teachings of the Holy Evangelists, and by kissing the Bible, but only by a 'yea,' or a little inclination of the head." It will be recalled that a clause in Penn's charter required all laws passed in the province to be submitted to the Privy Council of England for final approval. When, in obedience to this injunction, the enactment in question was transmitted it was promptly rejected by that transatlantic body. The measure, however, was not allowed to die. It was revived in 1714, and after much urging, after bringing considerable pressure to bear, ultimately received the approval of the Council three years later.

The great bugbear with which the Quaker government had to contend was the granting of supplies for military purposes. "My being many years in the Assembly, a majority of which were constantly Quakers," says Franklin, " gave me frequent opportunity of seeing the embarrassment given them by their principles against war, whenever application was made to them, by order of the crown, to grant aids for military purposes. They were unwilling to offend the government on the one hand, by direct refusal; and their friends, the body of the Quakers, on the other, by a compliance contrary to their principles; using a variety of evasions to avoid complying, and modes of disguising the compliance, when it became unavoidable. The common mode at last was, to grant money under the phrase of its being *for the King's use* and never to inquire how it was applied."[1]

This and similar pretenses of obtaining supplies appear to have been thoroughly worked by the different governors.[2]

---

[1] *Works*, Vol. I, pp. 153-4.

[2] May 16, 1693, Gov. Fletcher said to the Assembly, "If ther be anie amongst you that Scruple the giving of money to support warr, ther are a great manie other charges in that govermt, for the support yr of, as officers Sallaries & other Charges that amount to a Considerable sum ; your money shall be converted to these uses & shall not be dipt in blood."—*Col. Rec. of Pa.*, I, 361.

During the incumbency of Markham, for instance, the Assembly was requested to authorize the levy of a sum of money to be remitted to the Governor of New York for the support of war—or, as it was decently pretended, "for the relief of the distressed Indians."[1] The Assembly, on this presentation of the matter, voted £300 to be remitted to the neighboring province for the purpose therein specified. To keep up this pleasing and innocuous fiction, Governor Fletcher subsequently wrote to Markham informing him that the money had been faithfully expended in "feeding and clothing" the Indians. Had he replied the grant had been faithfully expended in purchasing bullets and other munitions of war, the letter would doubtless have approximated nearer the truth. But thus it was that the Quakers drew the line sharply between granting money for military purposes and for the support of the government. In their opinion, they were not answerable for the application of the supplies when once they had been granted. The responsibility was transferred *eo instanti* from them to the Governor.

In 1709 a concrete case occurred. Those were turbulent times, and the Governor of the Colony considered himself obliged to issue a requisition for troops and the necessary supplies. The story is told in his own words: "The Queen," writes Mr. Gookin, "having honored me with her commands that this Province should furnish out 150 men as its quota for the Expedition against Canada, I called on Assembly, and demanded £4000, they being all Quakers, after much delay, Resolved *nemine contradicente* that it was contrary to their religious principles to hire men to kill one another. I told some of them the Queen did not hire men to kill one another, but to destroy her enemies. One of them answered the Assembly understood English. After I had tried all ways to bring them to reason, they again resolved *nemine contradicente* that they could not directly or indirectly raise money for the

---

[1] Those of the Six Nations.

Expedition to Canada, but they had voted the Queen £500 as a Token of their respect, &c., and that the money should be put into a safe hand till they were satisfied from England it would not be employed to the use of war. I told them that the Queen did not want such a sum, but being a pious and good woman, perhaps she might give it to the clergy sent hither for the propagation of the Gospel. One of them answered that was worse than the other, on which arose a debate in the Assembly whether they should give the money or not, since it might be employed for the war or against their future Establishment, and after much wise debate it was carried in the affirmative by one voice only."[1]

A repetition of the same trouble was experienced when an attack was made upon Carthagena. The northern Colonies were called upon to furnish soldiers for that service, and Pennsylvania was appealed to among the number. The Assembly was composed almost exclusively of Friends, and the difficulty was how to obtain the necessary grant. The problem, however, was finally solved in a manner satisfactory to all. The Quakers discharged their duty by voting £4000 for the *King's use*, which signified, of course, that they would furnish the money, and the Governor should raise the soldiers on his own responsibility. It thus appears that the Quakers just reversed the popular adage, "Millions for defense, but not one cent for tribute." Evidently, in the opinion of the Society, the reformed maxim should read, "Millions for tribute, but not a cent for defense."

It is not very difficult to imagine that this granting of supplies occasionally brought the Friends into direct conflict with the Governors, who sometimes—and that frequently—represented a radically different line of thought from the one prevailing among the majority of the colonists. Governor Evans, in particular, had little respect for the Quaker *notions*, as he contemptuously styled them. He, for one, completely

---

[1] Letter to the Secretary, dated Phila., Aug. 27, 1709.

ignored their conscientious convictions and pacific policy. It was this man who for the first time in the history of the Province made a call by public proclamation for militia for the defence of the Colony. Many of the other Governors, however, were not unlike him. Mr. Gookin, as can easily be conjectured from the foregoing citation, was neither a votary of Quaker principles, nor a courtier of their special favor. Consequently he was incessantly involved in disputes, and in all sorts of litigation with the Quaker element of the community.

This want of sympathy on the part of the Governors led many of the inhabitants to look favorably on the assumption of the government of the Colony by the Crown. After the decease of William Penn affairs grew steadily worse. The Friends became more and more jealous and suspicious of the new proprietors. Many of these Quakers had fallen away or openly abandoned the doctrines of the Society, and desired to regulate the government solely according to their own interests and ideas. This accounts for the fact that we find the Quakers in 1755 strongly in favor of abolishing the proprietary government and establishing a royal one in its stead. It was then the general opinion of the Friends that "the powers of the government ought, in all good policy, to be separated from the power attending that immense property and lodge where they could be properly and safely lodged, in the hands of the king." The Proprietaries, however, manipulated the affair in such a way that the opposition gradually subsided and as a result the government remained practically unchanged.

The Pennsylvania colonists began to regard with uneasiness, not to say positive alarm, the ever increasing concourse of strangers differing from them in religion, as well as in other essential principles. This tide of immigration was considered portentous of evil. The Friends apprehended a preponderance of sentiments, other than their own, in the public councils, and finally, perhaps, an entire expulsion of all that tincture of

Quaker principles which they had been to so much trouble to infuse into the provincial policy and administration. Although these apprehensions, when viewed in the calm light of the nineteenth century, appear to have been considerably exaggerated, the record discloses the fact that such fears were not entirely without foundation. In the year 1729 no fewer than 6208 European settlers found their way into the Province of Pennsylvania. Even the Assembly took fright at such an unprecedented influx of foreigners. An ordinance was therefore hastily constructed entitled " An Act imposing a Duty on Persons convicted of heinous Crimes, & to prevent Poor and Impotent Persons from being imported into this Province." [1] By this statute a tax of five shillings *per capita* was imposed upon all new comers. It was not very long, however, before the provincial legislators became convinced of the impolicy of this measure. It was, therefore, soon repealed, and the Colony again extended a most cordial welcome to all who desired to find a home within its limits.

It will doubtless be remembered that one clause in the Charter granted to William Penn provided for the establishment of the English Church in Pennsylvania, when desired by twenty or more of the inhabitants. This provision also occasioned the Quakers some slight annoyance. A great many churchmen had followed them across the Atlantic, and had settled in the Colony. These individuals were not, as the Quakers had been, fleeing from persecution, but were as a rule, energetic, younger sons of good families—men belonging to the middle classes of society, those who had determined to secure better fortunes in America than England offered them. These persons soon became a prosperous and influential element in the Province. The churchmen were not members of the Society, and although in the main law abiding, they did not entirely agree with the administration, and frequently

---

[1] *Laws of Pa.*, I, 158.

expressed their opinions on the subject with a frankness that was nothing less than exasperating.

For some years, however, everything was sufficiently harmonious. But in 1695, the Bishop of London sent the Rev. Mr. Clayton to Philadelphia, and then the real trouble seems to have commenced. A gentleman[1] writing to Governor Markham affirms that the Quakers denounced the aforesaid Mr. Clayton as "the minister of the doctrines of devils," together with other language equally uncomplimentary, and that they behaved in various other scandalous ways. "His Majesty's Commission with the seal to it," our informant proceeds to say, they "held up in open court, in a ridiculous manner, shewing it to the people, and laughing at it, saying, 'Here is a baby in a Tin box—we are not to be frightened with babes.' And others have said, 'The King has nothing more to do here than to receive a bear skin or two yearly; and his, and the Parliament's laws reach no further than England, Wales, and the Town of Berwick upon the Tweed;' and such like expressions which can all be proved by sufficient Witnesses."

The churchmen in the Colony immediately presented a petition to the Crown, protesting against such heroic treatment. "The Quaker magistrate no sooner heard of it," continues the account of Mr. Suder, "but sent for me and the person that mentioned it, by a constable to their sessions. They told me they heard I with some others was petitioning his Majesty that we might have a minister of the Church of England for the exercise of our Religion and to make use of our arms as a Militia to defend our estates from enemies. Edward Shippen, one of the Quaker justices, turning to the others of his fellows say'd, 'Now they have discovered themselves. They are bringing the priest and the sword among us, but God forbid; we will prevent them,' and ordered the King's Attorney, a Quaker, to read a law that they had made against any person that shall

---

[1] A Mr. Suder, Nov. 20, 1698.

write or speak against their Government. I told them I hoped they would not hinder us of the right of petitioning "—and so the letter continues. Of course, due allowance should be made for the fact that this epistle was the composition of a churchman, one who would very naturally magnify any defect that existed in the Quaker Government. In all this, however, one thing is sufficiently apparent, to wit, that Pennsylvania was a state intended first of all for the Quakers. Its establishment had been for the primary purpose of affording this sect a haven of refuge. The Society, therefore, determined to retain the power of government in its own hands. In their fears, the Friends had no doubt greatly exaggerated the impending danger. They imagined that the Province was rapidly being populated by churchmen, and that if once the English church were to obtain the supremacy, they would be compelled to seek other homes or suffer another season of persecution. But after the excitement had somewhat subsided, the Quakers, whom, despite reports, history informs the reader never made any decided opposition to the new foundation, readily withdrew all their protests, and accordingly a branch of the Episcopal vine was planted in Pennsylvania.

Civil government, owing to their religious principles, was, however, always very embarrassing to the Friends. It became more and more so, as the population became more heterogeneous. Great difficulty was experienced in providing for the public defense of the Colony, and it became every day more apparent that the time was rapidly approaching when they would be compelled to lay down the government, consigning it to hands whose owners did not share such scruples.

The Quakers now perceived the impossibility of reconciling the preservation of their sectarian principles with the administration of the political power in the Colony which their ancestors had planted. But although they clearly recognized the inevitable, to which they saw they must eventually bow in submission, they were none the less reluctant to resign their power of control. History cannot censure them on this account. It had been principally with the hope of cultivating their tenets, and of exhibiting them to the world in a high degree of perfection that the Friends had originally incurred the lot of exiles from their native shores and been induced to undertake the care of government. In spite of this disinclination, however, the time had now arrived when some decision must be rendered. No longer was there any opportunity of halting between conflicting opinions. One of two things must be done. They must either renounce their political capacity, or they must consent to merge the Quaker into the politician. Which would be done? " With a rare virtue," avers Mr. Grahame, " they adhered to their religious principles and resigned the political authority which they had enjoyed since the foundation of the colony."[1]

Historical writers invariably find it an unsatisfactory process to endeavor to compress any great event within the narrow boundaries of chronological limits; especially is this true of a government like the one under consideration. It is, therefore, difficult to state *exactly* when this change occurred in Pennsylvania. Even the opinions of authorities differ as to what precise date is to be assigned to the crisis. Stillé alleges that the Quaker supremacy terminated in the year 1754.[2] Mr. Grahame goes a little further, assigning 1756 as the time. While McKean gives the date of the American Revolution as contemporary with the actual extinction of Quaker political power.

At all events, it would certainly be erroneous to suppose that this "rotation in office," so to speak, was effected suddenly, all at once—in a day, as the ancients were accustomed to found their cities. On the contrary, it was doubtless a very

---

[1] *Col. Hist. of U. S.*, II, 255.
[2] But it probably extended beyond this limit, for February 26, 1756, an argument was made before the Lords of Trade to forever disqualify Quakers from sitting as members of the Assembly. The petitioners declared that the pacific principles of the Friends conclusively demonstrated "the necessity of which we desire, namely, that they should be excluded from the Assembly. . . . These are the People, who impiously trust that the Lord will raise Walls & Bulwarks, round them, without their using any, the ordinary means, which he has put in their Power, for their own Preservation."

gradual process. A number of Quakers quietly seceded from the Assembly, declining to accept the offices of government under a political regime by which a military establishment was sanctioned, and indeed, even required. Their example was followed by other members of the Society, till, at first their majority was extinguished, and ultimately few, if any, Quakers remained in the Legislature.

Thus expired the political government of the Friends for and by the Friends. It had begun nearly a century before with exalted ideals. "In the whole," wrote the illustrious William Penn, "we aim at duty to the King, the preservation of rights to all, the suppression of vice and encouragement of virtue and arts, with liberty to all people to worship Almighty God according to their faith and persuasion." That it had accomplished all it proposed to do few denied, and in praise of it many have recorded their names. Dr. Franklin, for example, draws a very pleasing picture of the political household of Pennsylvania, when he likens it to "a father and his Family, the latter united by Interest and Affection, the former to be revered for the Wisdom of his Instruction and the indulgent Use of his Authority." "Nobody,' he adds, " was oppress'd ; Industry was sure of Profit, Knowledge of Esteem, and Virtue of Veneration."[1]

All impartial investigators will agree with the authority just cited that Quakerism always inscribed on its banner the device, "A free religion and a free commonwealth." Consequently the historian Lodge, who pays such a glowing, but deserved, tribute to this régime, simply expresses the verdict of history when he declares that "The oppression of New England and Virginia, of Congregationalist and Episcopalian, was unknown" in Pennsylvania, and that here "toleration did not rest on the narrow foundation of expediency to which it owed its early adoption in Maryland."[2]

---

[1] *Hist. Rev. of the Const. of Pa.*, p. 3.
[2] *Short Hist. of Eng. Col. in Amer.*, p. 233.

III.

Attitude of Quakers towards Indians.

The Indian policy of William Penn was a radical departure from the approved methods of his day and generation. As early as 1681, we discover the Proprietor of the future province directing his attention to the American natives. On the tenth day of October of that year, Penn appointed three Commissioners whose duty it was to supervise the settlement of the proposed colony. The instructions to these gentlemen were couched in the following language: "Be tender of offending the Indians, and hearken, by honest spies, if you can hear that anybody inveigles the Indians not to sell, or to stand off and raise the value upon you. . . . Let them know that you are come to sit down lovingly among them. Let my letter, and conditions with my purchasers about just dealing with them, be read in their tongue, that they may see we have their good in our eye, equal with our own interest, and after reading my letter and the said conditions, then present their kings with what I send them, and make a friendship and league with them, according to these conditions, which carefully observe, and get them to comply with you."[1]

The letter which accompanied these directions has become a famous document. In it Penn writes "there is one great God and power that hath made the world and all things therein, to whom you and I, and all people owe their being and well-being, and to whom you and I must one day give an

---

[1] Hazard, *Annals*, 529.

account for all that we do in the world; this great God hàth written His law in our hearts, by which we are taught and commanded to love and help, and do good to one another, and not to do harm and mischief one to another. Now this great God hath been pleased to make me concerned in your part of the world, and the king of the country where I live hath given unto me a great province, but I desire to enjoy it with your love and consent, that we may always live together as neighbors and friends." The author knows, so he proceeds to say, that the Indians have been greatly maltreated by some of the earlier European settlers, but assures them that he is "not such a man, as is well known" in his own country. Indeed, so far from entertaining such sentiments, the letter continues, I have "great love and regard towards you, and I desire to win and gain your love and friendship by a kind, just, and peaceable life, and the people I send are of the same mind, and shall in all things behave themselves accordingly; and if in anything any shall offend you or your people, you shall have a full and speedy satisfaction for the same, by an equal number of just men on both sides, that by no means you may have just occasion of being offended against them." The communication closes with the observation, " I shall shortly come to you myself, at what time we may more largely and freely confer and discourse of these matters."

This promise foreshadowed the treaty,[1] which, when Penn did arrive, was concluded under the famous Elm—the tree that has acquired such prominence in the history of the Province. And well it might, for one of the fairest and most unsullied chapters, perhaps, in the entire colonial history of America is that which describes this meeting with the aboriginal inhabitants. Here, translating into life their large and catholic theology, the Quakers met unarmed those same Indians, whom all the other European settlers agreed in regarding as fierce and

---

[1] This treaty has received the name of Elm Tree Treaty, because the meeting occurred in a grove of these trees.

blood-thirsty savages; and, addressing them as the children of a Common Father, one over-all-ruling God, concluded with them the memorable compact.

Other places have possessed their historic and consecrated trees, but none of them was ever more justly renowned than the Elm of Pennsylvania. It was a stately witness to the solemn covenant, which, in the language of Voltaire, was "the only league between those nations and the Christians that was never sworn to, and never broken." Here Penn explained to these rude children of the forest that he had not come to injure or to defraud them of their natural rights; that, on the contrary, his purpose was to ameliorate their condition; and, that for the accomplishment of this desired object, the interests of the races were to be considered inseparable—in fact, identical. "We meet," such was the language employed, "on the broad pathway of good faith and good will; no advantage shall be taken on either side, but all shall be openness and love." Further, he " would not do as the Marylanders did; that is, call them children or brothers only; for often parents were apt to whip their children too severely; and brothers sometimes would differ." Neither would he compare the friendship between them to a "chain, for the rain might sometime rust it, or a tree might fall and break it;" but he would "consider them as the same flesh and blood with the Christians; the same as if one man's body were to be divided into two parts." So terminates a declaration whose influence was clearly perceptible throughout the entire colonial period. The hearts of the congregated chiefs of the Algonquin race were immediately captured by the simplicity and evident sincerity of Penn's manner, as well as by the language of fraternal affection in which he had addressed them. On their part, therefore, they pledged themselves, in the glowing imagery of nature, to live with the children of Onas[1] "as long as the sun and moon shall endure."

---

[1] "Which signifies a Pen in the language of the Five Nations, by which name they call the Governors of Pennsylvania since it was first settled by William Penn." *Col. Rec. of Pa.*, II, 210.

Recognizing the abuses that had been committed by his predecessors, Penn declared that no person in his Colony would be permitted to defraud or otherwise injure the Indians, or even to avenge any wrong, real or imaginary, he might receive at their hands. Instead of killing the natives in case of altercation or an injury inflicted, Penn prescribed that if "any Indian should abuse a planter, the said planter should not be his own judge upon the Indian, but apply to the next magistrate, who should make complaint thereof to the king of the Indians, for reasonable satisfaction for the injury."[1] It was provided, moreover, that the adjustment of all disputes between the two races should in every instance be referred to twelve arbiters selected equally from the Europeans and the Indians. It was also declared that "the Indians shall have liberty to do all things relating to improvement of their ground, and providing sustenance for their families, that any of the planters shall enjoy." At the same time it was announced "that no man shall by any ways or means, in word or deed, affront or wrong any Indian, but he shall incur the same penalty of the law as if he had committed against his fellow planters." This language was repeated almost verbatim, April 23, 1701. Then it was agreed that the natives should "have the full and free privilege and immunities of all the said laws as any other Inhabitant."[2]

In the year 1728, the Governor informed the aborigines, "if any Christian do Injury to an Indian, you must as Brethren, come and complain of it ; but if it be remote in the Woods, you must apprehend the Man that did the Wrong, and deliver him to me, that the Offender may be punished for it according to our Laws, which will suffer no man to hurt another."[3]

The historian Herodotus relates of a certain Scythian tribe that "no man does any injury to this people, for they are accounted sacred ; nor do they possess any warlike weapons."[4]

---

[1] *Instructions to Colonists.*   [2] *Col. Rec.*, II, 10.
[3] *Ibid.*, III, 356.   [4] Bk. IV, chap. 23.

Notwithstanding the fact that these words were written many ages anterior to the period now under consideration, no phraseology could be found that better describes the relation existing between the Quakers and the Indians. Carnage held high court in many colonies. Indeed, even in some sections of Pennsylvania, devastation was rampant; but, in spite of this terror that stalked at noonday, the Friends, throughout their entire history, disclaimed the employment of all weapons, as well for the defence of their lives and property as for the redress of their wrongs. Their trust for the safety of their persons and possessions against human ferocity and cupidity was not in arms, but in the dominion of the Almighty over the hearts of His creatures; for, in the beautiful language of Inspiration, they firmly believed that "under His shadow" they might live even "among the heathen."[1]

Of this child-like faith and simplicity we possess a very striking instance. A family of Pennsylvania Quakers, although residing on the frontiers of the settlement, were accustomed to retire at night without even pulling in the latch-string of their dwelling, relying solely on God's providence to protect them. One evening, however, after the Indians had committed several atrocities in the immediate neighborhood, the good man of the house, before going to rest for the night, took the precaution to draw in the string. But the circumstance troubled his mind. Finally he arose from his bed, replaced the latch-string in its usual position, and as the sequel will show, this simple action proved the salvation of the entire family. Shortly afterwards the Indians surrounded the dwelling, tried the door, found the string out, and after a consultation of a few moments, retired, leaving the peaceable Friends unmolested. Subsequently, when peace was restored, the same Quaker happened to be in company with several natives, and related his experience. One of the Indians declared that the simple circumstance of putting out the latch-string, which proved

---

[1] *Lamentations*, iv, 20.

confidence rather than fear, had caused life as well as property to be spared. The speaker acknowledged that he himself had been one of that same marauding party, and that, on finding the door of the house unfastened, they had said, "these people shall live; they will do us no harm, for they put their trust in the Great Spirit." [1]

Whatever animosity the Indians might conceive against the European neighbors of the Pennsylvanians, or even against the colonists themselves, who were not included in the fold of the Society, they never failed to discriminate in favor of the followers of Penn. During all the time of border war when rumors of hostilities filled so many pages of colonial history, the natives, though in many cases urged on by unprincipled white men to commit deeds of violence, never molested the Friends—the people of Father Onas as they fondly styled them. Secretary Logan could then with truthfulness tell the Indians "You on your part have been faithful and true to us, whatever Reports might be spread, yet the Chain was still preserved strong and bright. You never violated it. We have lived in perfect Peace and Unity above any other Government in America." [2]

The condition of affairs herein described is really a remarkable phenomenon in the colonial life of America, but the reason for it is hidden only a little way beneath the surface. The Quaker principles and practices, their brotherly love, their rejection of weapons—all this made from the very beginning an impression, strong and enduring, upon the savage mind, and it is mainly to the circumstances enumerated that this notable exemption is to be attributed. The Quakers "in the midst of a fierce and lawless race of men," writes the annalist Burke, "have preserved themselves, with unarmed hands and passive principles, by the rules of moderation and justice better than any other people by policy and arms." [3] "No feature," con-

---

[1] *Harper's Mag.*, I, 596.
[2] *Col. Rec. of Pa.*, III, 88.
[3] *Europ. Set. in America*, II, 227.

firms Mr. Grahame, "in the manners of the Quakers contributed more efficiently to guard them against Indian ferocity than their rigid abstinence not merely from the use, but even from the possession, of offensive weapons, enforced by their conviction of the sufficiency of divine aid, and their respect to the Scriptural threat, that all who take the sword shall perish by it."[1]

Throughout the whole period of Indian wars there were, as far as the writer's knowledge extends, only two cases where Friends were massacred by the savages, and these resulted from misunderstandings. The first was that of a young man, a tanner by trade, who went to and from his tannery daily without being molested while devastation spread in every direction. On one occasion, however, he carried a gun to shoot some birds. He was seen by the Indians. They imagined the weapon was carried for protection against them, and without further ado he was murdered. The other instance was the case of a woman, who remained in her dwelling unharmed, although her neighbors were cruelly massacred. The ravages of the Indians were, however, so frightful, that she finally became alarmed, and fled to the adjoining fort to ensure her personal safety. The savages supposed she had abandoned her pacific principles. They inferred from her conduct that she had allied herself with the fighting portion of the community, and her life paid the forfeit. But with the exception of these instances the records remain untarnished. Indeed, so free are they from such blemishes that Mr. Grahame possesses ample authority when, by way of recapitulation, he declares that "the intentional injury of a Quaker by an Indian" was "an event almost, if not altogether, unknown in Pennsylvania, and very rare in all American history."[2]

In the annals of Pennsylvania, then, one does not encounter pages which are blotted and seared by inhuman conduct towards the Indians, nor by exhibitions of deadly animosity

---

[1] *Col. Hist. of U. S.*, I, 515–16.   [2] *Col. History of U. S.*, I, 515.

on the part of the aborigines towards the Friends. Penn, in his letter, had given every assurance that no advantage would be taken of them; that all the transactions between the two races were to be characterized by equity and brotherly love. These statements were not intended merely to deceive. Almost immediately upon the arrival of the Proprietor abundant verification was afforded of the promises made to the red men; and one of Penn's first acts was to obtain the natives' consent to the occupation of their country. To be sure the Province had been granted by the King in absolute right, and the title to the territory thus conferred was such as was considered valid by all nations, but when Penn determined to add the additional right of purchase from the original owners, he made a very favorable impression on the sachems. The chronicler Chalmers alleges that before Penn's departure from England, several conversations relative to this subject were held with the Bishop of London, and that the former was notably influenced by the opinion of his ecclesiastical friend, who advised him to pursue this meritorious policy. Investigation fails to discover any authority in substantiation of this statement, but whether the assertion be veracious or otherwise is not material for our present purpose. Suffice it to say that, no matter whence the idea originated, Penn carried it into successful operation, and that the result went far to constitute the most honorable feature in the colonial history of America. It is the same Chalmers who declares that this conduct, "equally humane and wise, not only long ensured an advantageous peace to the province, but has conferred undiminished celebrity on his name;"[1] and the historian Burke, when speaking on the same subject, states that by this "act of justice at the beginning, he made his dealings for the future the more easy, by prepossessing the Indians with a favorable opinion of him and his designs."[2]

But Penn did not stop here. Creditable as this conduct may have been, it was by no means unique, for it was only

---

[1] *Annals*, p. 644.   [2] *Europ. Set. in America*, II, 227.

one instance, among many, of the illustrious deeds of this Quaker Patriarch. The matter of trade with the natives furnishes another example; and, in this respect, his conduct was marked by as great, if not greater, scrupulousness. In 1681, although in considerable pecuniary need, he unhesitatingly refused an offer of £6000, together with a handsome annual revenue, for a monopoly of the Indian traffic, because, as Penn wrote to a friend, "I could not so defile what comes to me clean." In the same year it was officially declared, "Forasmuch as it is usual with the planters to overreach the poor natives of the country in Trade by Goods not being good of the kind, or debased with mixtures, with which they are sensibly aggrieved, it is agreed, whatever is sold to the Indians, in consideration of their furs, shall be sold in the market place, and there suffer the test, whether good or bad; if good to pass; if not good, not to be sold for good, that the natives may not be abused nor provoked."

Twelve years later, that is in 1693, on complaint being made to the effect that traveling traders "who by reason of their Non-Residence as aforesaid and frequent Removal from one province to another, are not careful in maintaining a fair Correspondence with the sd. Indians, and often oppress and abuse them in their way of trading and dealing with them, which may provoke and stir up the sd. Indians to a Revenge of the said abuses," it was enacted, "that no person non-Resident, either on Shoar or on board any vessel (except such as Come here with their families with an Intent to settle) deal or trade with any Indians within this government, upon any pretence whatsoever, upon the forfeiture of five pounds for every such offence and the goods so purchased, one half to go to the use of the County and the other to the discoverer." It was provided further that "no Inhabitant within this Province and Territories from henceforth under the penalty aforesaid, shall presume to trade with the Indians in the woods, at their towns or wigwams, after any private or clandestine manner, but at their respective mansion houses, which sd. dwelling houses shall be adjudged so to be by the respective Court in each county, any law, custom or usage to the contrary notwithstanding."[1]

At many meetings of the Governor and his Council, Indian matters were discussed, and measures were early taken to suppress, or, if this were impossible, at least to regulate, the sale of intoxicating liquors to the natives. Such commerce had already become a prolific source of anxiety as well as annoyance to the Friends; and, if it were allowed to continue, they clearly perceived that the prospect for the future would not be the most attractive possible. Despite all efforts to the contrary, however, spirituous drinks still found their way among the tribes. In 1701, to suppress this fountain-head of crime, a law was framed declaring "that no Rum shall be Sold to any but their Chiefs, and in such Quantities as the Govr and Council shall think fitt, to be Disposed of by the Said Chiefs to the Indians about them as they shall see cause."[2] By such means the traffic was diminished, but not abolished. Other expedients must be tried. June 22, 1715, therefore, it was ordered on the authority of "the Govr and Council, that all Indians who shall at any time see any rum brought amongst them for sale, either by English or others, Do forthwith stave ye Casks and destroy the Liquor, without suffering any of it to be sold or Drank, in wch Practice they shall be Indemnified and protected by ye Govmt against all persons whatsoever."[3] But this was expecting too much of crude humanity and the measure remained a nullity. The Indians were entirely too fond of "fire water" to pursue any such course as the one proposed. In order, therefore, the better to accomplish the desired result, a lengthy bill was passed in the year 1722 entitled "An Act to prohibit the selling Rum, and other strong Liquors, to the *Indians*, and to prevent the abuses that may happen thereby." The phraseology of many sec-

---

[1] Linn, *Charter and Laws of Pa.*, pp. 240-1.
[2] *Col. Rec. of Pa.*, II, 16.   [3] *Ibid.*, II, 633.

tions of this statute is extremely curious. For instance, the enactment declared that nothing therein contained should "be deemed or taken to prevent any Inhabitant of this Province from giving unto any *Indian*, at his Dwelling house, or Habitation, any Quantity of Rum, or other spirits, not exceeding One Sixteenth Part of a Quart at one Time, and that not oftener than once in Twelve Hours."[1] Even at this early date some of the Quakers appear to have classified alcohol with other medicinal remedies, and would have administered it accordingly in homœopathic doses. But, unfortunately, the natives entertained quite the contrary opinion concerning its uses.

In all his transactions with the Indians, Penn never abandoned the policy he had outlined in his treaty and his officers were always strictly enjoined to treat their heathen neighbors as they themselves had been treated by their Governor. There was seldom any difference noticeable between their actions towards their fellows and the savages, whom they regarded as their wards. To be convinced of this fact one does not have to turn many leaves of the records. Examples almost everywhere appear.

The following incident will suffice for the purposes of concrete illustration: In the year 1721, two traders became involved in a dispute with a party of Indians. Blows quickly followed angry words, and finally, in the heat of the altercation, one of the Indians was killed. Notwithstanding the fact that this act of violence was committed far away from the abodes of civilization—in an almost impenetrable forest—the Governor of Pennsylvania sent out officers to apprehend the transgressors, and the record affirms that they "were brought to Philadelphia, committed to prison and put in Irons, and there remain to be tried for their Lives according to our Laws, in the same manner as if they had killed an Englishman."[2] When, however, the Indians discovered that the

---

[1] *Laws of Pa.*, 117–18.   [2] *Col. Rec. of Pa.*, III, 205.

affair "happened by misfortune," they considered "it hard the persons who killed our friend and Brother should suffer," and at their earnest solicitation that "the men who did it may be released from Prison and set at Liberty," the traders were pardoned.[1] As already remarked, however, there is nothing exceptional about this case. It should always be remembered that during the time of Quaker supremacy, individuals were punished in precisely the same manner for the injuries inflicted on Indians as for similar offences committed against Europeans.

Throughout their entire history, the Quakers were careful not to offend the natives in any respect. In the early part of the last century it was customary for vessels to fire salutes, thereby indicating their arrival or departure; to welcome their friends on board; or for similar reasons, and this was done several times in the harbor of Philadelphia. The Indians, however, "believing ye firing of sd. guns to have been signs of Hostilitie intended ag^t y^m," were very much frightened by such warlike demonstrations. It was, therefore, promptly ordered that the practice of discharging cannons in the city or harbor be discontinued. To retain the good opinion of the natives, the Governor hastened to explain to their representatives "that itt was the Custom of ye English to fire guns as a sign of joy & kind entertainment of y^r friends coming on board; & was in no manner of ways intended to frighten or disoblige y^m; as also informed y^m y^t they were & should be verie wellcome to this gov^{r}m^t, and in token of amitie & friendship wt y^m, ye Govr gave y^m a Belt of Wampum, by y^m to be showen to the other Seneca Indians y^t went away upon fireing ye said guns."[2] In the year 1712, also, when a delegation of natives complained that their corn had been greatly damaged by the traders carelessly allowing their cattle to get into it, the offenders were compelled to furnish a satisfactory indemnity to the injured parties.[3]

---

[1] *Ibid.*, III, 211.
[2] *Col. Rec. of Pa.*, I, 557. [3] *Ibid.*, II, 519–20.

As time wore away, representatives of other denominations began to settle in the colony; but, as they rejected the peaceable ways of their neighbors, they naturally enjoyed no exemption from Indian warfare. They had sown the wind and they soon found that the whirlwind must be reaped. In spite of all admonitions to the contrary, they took the sword and as a result many of them perished by it. When it was too late, they perceived that by themselves they were no match for the superior numbers of the Indians. Attempts, therefore, were made to induce the Quakers to waive their religious scruples, and to take up arms for the defense of the Province. As might be expected, however, such efforts were utterly futile.

About the year 1705, Governor Evans determined to test the sincerity of the Friends in this matter, and he did it in rather a discreditable manner, a way that reflected as little honor on him as on his coadjutors. To accomplish his purpose, however, this officer caused reports to be widely circulated to the effect that the Indians were devastating the surrounding country, and that an immediate attack on the City of Philadelphia was to be apprehended. So far as the Quakers were concerned the experiment was entirely useless in securing the result which the Governor most desired. In this, their hour of trial, they remained steadfast. The time selected was the day on which they were accustomed to hold their regular weekly meeting, and, regardless of the tumult and consternation that pervaded the settlement, the majority of the Friends quietly assembled as usual to perform their appointed devotions. Of course, in any large body of persons, complete unanimity of action is not to be expected. Some individuals were disconcerted owing to the unexpectedness of the affair and the vivid descriptions of the terrible cruelties being perpetrated in the neighborhood. "The suddenness of the surprise," such are the words of the historian Proud, "with the noise of precipitation, consequent thereon, threw many of the people into very great fright and consternation, inasmuch that it is said, some threw their plate and most valuable effects down their wells and little-houses; that others hid themselves, in the best manner they could, while many retired further up the river, with what they could most readily carry off."[1] With a thrill of pardonable pride, however, our author adds that only four Quakers were induced to arm themselves to repel the expected attack.

Through evil as well as through good report, the Friends continued firm in their pacific principles in general, and concerning their attitude towards the Indians they were literally immovable. As would be naturally supposed their conduct in this respect occasioned a great deal of trouble from the opposition; but, no matter how severe and dogged this persecution might be, the members of the Society persisted in allegiance to their religious convictions. After Braddock's memorable defeat, there was great commotion in Pennsylvania owing to apprehensions of the hostility of the enraged natives. With the exception of the adherents of the Society, the community united in advocating defensive measures. Those individuals residing on the frontier were incessantly inundating the Assembly with petitions for assistance. When it was ascertained, however, that all such attempts were perfectly idle, they resorted to intimidation, and threatened to come down in great crowds and cut the obdurate Governor and his advisers limb from limb, if steps were not taken, and that speedily, for what they considered the proper defense of the community. But these barbarous menaces were just as ineffectual as their former efforts, and when it was so discovered, a new device, novel in character, was adopted. In order to move the Quakers from their detested pacific policy, it was determined, as a last resource, to convey to Philadelphia the bodies of a whole family that had been recently massacred by the Indians. The record states that the remains really did arrive in the city like "frozen venison," for it was midwinter. They were paraded through the town and finally deposited in front of the Legislative Hall,

---

[1] *Hist. of Pa.*, Vol. I, pp. 469-70.

where the law-makers could see for themselves the fiendish work of the savages. John Churchman, an eye witness of this spectacle, reports that the bodies "were carried along the streets—many people following, cursing the Indians, and also the Quakers, because they would not join in war for their destruction." These were indeed trying times for Friends. Experimental knowledge had, however, thoroughly convinced them that confidence in the Supreme Ruler of events was far better protection than a resort to arms. After thoughtful consideration, therefore, the only reply the Society vouchsafed to these menaces and hostile demonstrations was made in the language of the Scripture—"Fear not them that kill the body."

In the very teeth of fierce opposition, the Friends maintained their peaceable relations with the natives—relations which, from the very beginning, had assumed a very practical form. Mutual assistance appears to have been the dominant idea. Richard Townsend, the personal friend of William Penn, records the fact that "as our worthy proprietor treated the Indians with extraordinary humanity they became very civil and loving to us, and brought in abundance of venison." Penn on his part, says Mr. Bancroft, "often met the Indians in council, and at their festivals. He visited them in their cabins, shared the hospitable banquet of hominy and roasted acorns, and laughed, and frolicked, and practiced athletic games with the light-hearted, mirthful, confiding red men."[1]

This friendship between the two races was so strong that Indians frequently came to visit socially, and even to live among the Quakers. Under such conditions, the influence exerted on them was very salutary, for here they acquired useful ideas regarding civilization which in time inured to the great profit of their people. The Indians were not slow either in recognizing the superior qualities of the Europeans and to argue from the kind treatment received that the

---

[1] *Hist. of U. S.*, II, 384.

Quakers were in reality their best councilors. In conversation, therefore, Philadelphia was frequently referred to as "their head;" thus symbolizing, under natural imagery, that the City of Brotherly Love was even greater than their chief, that to a great extent it directed and controlled their actions. On more than one occasion did the natives publicly declare that they gave no credence to damaging reports against the Friends, for they claimed complete identity with the people of Father Onas. If proof of this statement be required, it is found in a speech delivered by an Indian chief in the year 1715. He says, "that hearing of some murmurs among some of themselves, to prevent any misunderstanding, they now came to renew the former bond of friendship. That William Penn had, at his first coming, made a clear & open Road all the way to the Indians (by this meaning a friendly communication), that they desired the same might be kept open, and that all obstructions should be removed, of wch on their sides they will take care." In conclusion the speaker assured his audience that he earnestly desired "the Indians should be half English & the English make themselves as half Indians," so that "they should be joyn'd as one." [1]

Numerous indeed were the Indians who bore testimony to the fact that they never received any other than good counsel from the Quakers, advice of such a character that it was always to their advantage to follow it implicitly. At an Indian council convened in the year 1720, the members almost unanimously declared they would always remember the words of their great and good brother, William Penn. They stated that since their chiefs had come in contact with the Quakers they had lived in almost uninterrupted tranquillity. "When the sun sets"—such was their language—"we sleep in peace; in peace we rise with him, and so continue while he continues in his course, and think ourselves happy in their friendship, which we shall take care to have continued from generation to generation."

---

[1] *Col. Rec. of Pa.*, Vol. II, pp. 628–29.

On another occasion, the Indians also assured the Governor that their relations with the Friends were a source of real satisfaction to them. They said: " We are happy to live in a Country at Peace, and not as in those Parts, where we formerly Liv'd; for then upon our Return from hunting, We found our Town surprized and our Women and children taken prisoners by our Enemies."[1] They perceived that "he that withholds his hand from war is wise;" and the Quakers, on their part, neglected few opportunities of farther impressing the unquestionable advantages of peace on the plastic minds of their red brethren. In the year 1719, for instance, the Friends expressed their hopes that the natives were "all fully convinced that Peace is better than War, which destroys you and will bring you nothing; your strong young People being first killed, the old Women and Children are left defenseless, who soon will become a Prey. And so all the nation perishes without leaving a name to Posterity." Moreover, logically argued the Quakers, this advice of itself was an unmistakable indication that we are your true friends, for if we were not then we "should encourage you to Destroy one another. For Friends save People from Ruin and Destruction, but Enemies destroy them."[2]

From this *résumé* it will be sufficiently evident that the actions of the Quakers relative to the Indians were invariably characterized by equity. In the light of facts, the verdict of the impartial historian must ever coincide with that expressed by the Friends themselves when they alleged, we have done better "than if, with the proud Spanards, we had gained the mines of Potosi. We may make the ambitious heroes, whom the world admires, blush for their shameful victories. To the poor, dark souls round about us we teach their rights as men."[3]

---

[1] *Col. Rec. of Pa.*, II, 403.   [2] *Ibid.*, III, 71.
[3] *Planter's Speech*, 1684. Quoted by Bancroft, II, 383.

IV.

ATTITUDE OF QUAKERS TOWARDS SLAVERY.

Originally, the actions of the Society with respect to the purchase and retention of slaves, differed but little from the ways of colonists of other religious persuasions. The reasons are obvious. The early Pennsylvanians possessed large allotments of land without a sufficient number of laborers for proper cultivation; they had large families without an adequate number of servants for the necessary domestic employment. It was only natural therefore that the Friends directed their attention to the negro as a means of supplying the existing deficiency. As Mr. Grahame observes, "it required more virtue than even the Quakers were yet prepared to exert, in order to defend them from the contagion of this evil."[1]

During Penn's first visit to the Colony, a few blacks were imported into Pennsylvania. Subsequently Africans were literally poured into the Province to obviate the difficulties resulting from the scarcity of labor, and they were bought promiscuously by all—indifferently, by the Quakers and by the members of other denominations. William Penn, following the fashion set by his neighbors, purchased slaves without much thought concerning the matter, except perhaps to make the yoke comparatively easy. Of this statement we possess documentary proof. In a letter[2] to his steward, Penn tells that gentlemen, after discoursing on the subject of domestics,

---

[1] *Col. Hist. U. S.*, Vol. I, p. 535.   [2] *Letters to his Steward*, 1685.

"it were better they were blacks, for then we might have them for life."

The first public act of the Proprietory relating to the negroes in his possession was simply to substitute the condition of adscripts to the soil for that of serfdom after fourteen years' service. At a later day he endeavored to secure to the Africans mental and moral culture, the rights and pleasures of domestic life. But these efforts to ameliorate their condition were only partially successful, and history tells us that William Penn died a slave owner. Had his life been prolonged, the narrative might have been different. For some time anterior to his decease, his mind had been gradually settling down to the conviction that it was morally wrong to own slaves, and his will contained provision for the emancipation of the negroes in his possession. "I give," he writes in one section of the document in question, "my blacks their freedom as is under my hand already, and to old Sam, 100 acres, to be his childrens' after he and his wife are dead, forever."

Although many Friends were thus engaged in purchases of this description, yet those constitutional principles, which belonged to the Society, caused its members to treat those whom they retained in their possession "with tenderness," considering them in practice as well as in theory brethren, for whose spiritual welfare especially it was well to be concerned. The Friends, although they had not yet reached the objective point of manumitting their negroes, had always regarded them as human beings, and had ever favored all attempts to impart to them religious instruction. As can well be imagined such efforts never failed to excite alarm among slave owners. Many early enactments clearly reveal this consternation. Of course, legal expression could not be obtained for such a sentiment in Pennsylvania, but in some colonies it secured formal statement in legislative measures. In the Barbadoes, for instance, an act was passed in the year 1676, prohibiting " the people called Quakers from bringing their negroes into their meetings for worship," even if these services were conducted in their own residences. The preamble of the statute attempts to furnish extenuation for this conduct by alleging that whereas, many negroes have been suffered to remain at the meeting of Quakers as hearers of their doctrine, and taught in the principles, " that hereby the safety of this island may be much hazarded;" and the body of the enactment declares that all such action should be severely punished under the criminal law of the land. This kindness of the Friends towards their blacks contributed very largely to draw a vail over the iniquity and more repulsive features of the institution. Watson in his " Annals " testifies to the fact. This writer affirms that the slaves of Philadelphia, " were a happier class of people than the free blacks." Harsh treatment was frowned down by the weight of public opinion, and if it occurred, the offender was practically ostracised in consequence. The same punishments were meted out to criminals, irrespective of color distinctions; and the murder of a slave was always punishable with the death penalty. In short, slavery, barring of course the power legally belonging to it, was in general little more than servitude. But even kind treatment did not fulfil all the requirements of the situation. Quakerism was essentially a democratic system; no rank could be acknowledged. Its members were all subjects of one Supreme Sovereign—the Lord of lords, and the King of kings; consequently the relation of slave and master was diametrically opposed to one of the most esteemed articles in their doctrinal belief. Notwithstanding, therefore, the undeniable fact that the slaves were ordinarily well treated by their owners, it did not deter certain individuals from becoming uneasy about retaining human beings in slavery of any sort. Even at this early time to such persons the slave trade was the greatest bane in their colonial existence.

Amongst the echoes from those distant years, we frequently catch the sounds of sympathy for the enslaved—a commiseration gradually assuming the tangible form of condemning the retention of slaves at all, no matter what treatment they received, be it harsh or mild. As early as the year 1688, some emigrants from Kresheim, Germany, who had adopted the principles of Penn, followed him across the Atlantic, and located at Germantown, entered their earnest protest against slavery, urging the inconsistency with the principles of the Christian religion of buying, selling, and holding men in bondage. Their memorial was illustrated in a very forcible manner. The petitioners argued that it was decidedly worse for professed Christians to possess slaves than for the Turks to enslave Christians, the one calling themselves by the name of Jesus; the other making no pretensions of following the meek and lowly Nazarene. "In Europe there are many oppressed for conscience sake; and here there are those oppressed which are of a black color." Moreover, when it should be reported abroad that the "Quakers do here handel men as they handel there the cattle," it would inevitably bring the Society into disrepute. Besides, the Friends were reminded that this iniquitous traffic caused almost incessant wars in Africa to supply the demand, and this fact was emphasized as an additional reason why the system *in toto* should receive their unqualified condemnation and strenuous opposition.

The document was first submitted to the Monthly Meeting. This body having duly considered its contents, declared "we find it so weighty that we think it not expedient for us to meddle with it here, but do rather commit it to y° consideration of y° Quarterly Meeting; y° tenor of it being nearly related to y° Truth." "It being a thing of too great a weight" for the Quarterly Meeting "to determine, the matter was recommended to the Yearly Meeting." By this assembly, "it was adjudged not to be so proper for this meeting to give a Positive Judgment in the case, It having so general a Relation to many other Parts, and therefore at present they forbear it."

And so for the time the affair rested. Popular opinion, however, was now thoroughly aroused, and from this time dates the inauguration of the Quaker crusade against the institution of slavery. The petition just mentioned was only the entering wedge of a struggle that after many years of patient and laborious contest, terminated in a way that cannot fail to redound to the honor of the Society.

In compliance with the suggestion offered by the residents of Germantown, the Friends almost immediately passed a resolution declaratory of the unlawfulness of slavery. But this did not satisfy many persons who were now seriously cogitating upon this important subject. In the year 1693, both the "Apostates" and the "Christian Quakers,"[1] while at variance on several points, united in stating, in the most trenchant language, their abiding belief in the unrighteousness of an institution that elevated one man by depressing his fellow-creature. At this time earnest exhortation and caution were given to all the members of the Society concerning the purchase and retention of negroes—the essence of this admonition being, that, in the future, no one was to buy blacks except with the purpose of liberation.

The first really official action of the Society in regard to trading in slaves, however, appears to have been taken by the Philadelphia Yearly Meeting of 1696. After prolonged meditation, this assembly issued the following injunction to its constituents: "Whereas, several papers have been read relating to the keeping and bringing in of negroes, which being duly considered, it is the advice of this Meeting that the Friends be careful not to encourage the bringing in of any more negroes; and that such that have negroes, be careful of them, bring them to meetings with them in their families, and restrain them from loose and lewd living as much as in them lies, and from rambling abroad on First days or other times." But no more immediate effect resulted from this measure than an increased concern for the spiritual welfare of the slaves, who, in many instances, were permitted to attend divine worship in the same meeting-houses with their Quaker masters.

---

[1] Appellatives invented by George Keith to describe his opponents and followers respectively.

Such then was the state of affairs in the year 1700, when William Penn left England and again returned to Pennsylvania. It was with great sorrow that the Proprietary perceived that negro slavery in his beloved Colony exhibited, in some instances, the same hideous features that characterized that barbarous institution in other geographical sections. He informs us that his "mind had long been engaged" for the benefit of the subject race, and with the purpose of ameliorating their condition, he introduced two bills into the Assembly. The first, concerned principally with the morals of the slaves, was rejected; the second, regulating their trials and punishments, was passed. Through this action of the Assembly, Penn's attempts to improve the condition of the bondsmen by legal enactments were rendered partially inoperative. But his zeal in the good cause was by no means abated. The following excerpt, extracted from the minutes of the Monthly Meeting, affords ample testimony to his solicitude for the welfare of those in bondage: "Our dear Friend and Governor having laid before this Meeting a concern that hath laid upon his mind for some time concerning the negroes and Indians, that Friends ought to be very careful in discharging a good conscience towards them in all respects, but more especially for the good of their souls, and that they might, as frequent as may be, come to meetings upon First-days, upon consideration whereof this Meeting concludes to appoint a meeting for the negroes, to be kept once a month, etc., and that their masters give notice thereof in their own families, and be present with them at the said meetings as frequent as may be."

From this quotation, it becomes sufficiently evident that at this period of their history, the Quakers, as a denomination, seemed to have been more anxious for the moral instruction of the slaves than for their immediate emancipation. Weighty measures, however, require decades for maturity. The popular mind must be prepared; vicious habits eradicated; prejudices conquered; in short, innumerable obstacles of every sort removed. It was so in the instance we are now examining. First came the blade; then the ear; finally, the full corn in the ear. We must not, therefore, expect to find *all* the Quakers instantly severing every connection with this iniquitous business. By keeping this fact well in mind we are prepared to interpret correctly some of the enactments, which, without such guidance, would be wholly inexplicable. Thus while the majority of the Friends were conscientious in their relations towards their slaves—notoriously lenient in their treatment of them, some harsh measures were not unknown in Pennsylvania, as is clearly demonstrated by the early legislation of that period.

In 1705, for example, an "Act for the Trial and Punishment of Negroes," became law. By its provisions, lashes were inflicted for petty offences, and death for crimes of greater magnitude. "If any Negro or Negroes within this Province," such is the phraseology, "shall commit a Rape or Ravishment upon any white Woman or Maid, or shall commit Murder, Buggery or Burglary, they shall be tried as aforesaid, and shall be punished with death." For an attempted rape "and for robbing, stealing or fraudulently taking and carrying away any goods, living or dead, above the value of Five Pounds, every Negroe, upon Conviction of any of the said Crimes, shall be whipped with Thirty-nine Lashes, and branded in the Forehead with the Letter R or T, and exported out of this Province by the Master or Owner, within Six months after conviction, never to return into the same, upon Pain of Death, and shall be kept in Prison till Exportation at their Masters, or Owners, or their own charge."[1] Slaves were not allowed to carry weapons without a special license, and if they violated this regulation they were to be whipped, receiving twenty-one lashes. It was declared unlawful for more than four to meet together, lest they might form cabals, conspiracies or riots. They were to be whipped, also, if discovered abroad after nine o'clock at night without a pass.

---

[1] *Laws of Pa.*, Vol. I, pp. 45-6.

In 1707, two slaves were condemned to death, "for Burglary proved ag'st them." But as there existed no provision in the government " for a Competent restitution to the Owners who loose their Slaves by the hand of Public Justice," it was resolved that the death penalty should be remitted under the following conditions: that the slaves should "be led from the Market place, up y[e] Second Street, & down thro' the front street to y[e] Bridge, with their arms extended & tied to a pole across their Necks, a Cart going before them, and that they shall be severely Whipt all the way as they pass, upon the bare back and shoulders; this punishment shall be repeated for 3 Market days successively; in the mean time they shall lie in Irons, in the prison, at the Owners Charge, until they have such an Opportunity as shall best please them for transportation."[1]

In 1711, the Friends determined to take a firm stand for the accomplishment of their final object. It was then that the introduction of slaves was strictly prohibited. The measure, however, being submitted to the Privy Council of England for assent, was promptly rejected by that body. The Quakers, although discouraged, were not cast down. In 1712, upon the presentation of a petition signed by many hands, they endeavored to accomplish their cherished object by assessing the large sum of £20 per capita on every slave subsequently imported into Pennsylvania. Progress ever begets progress and it was not long before this document evoked another still more aggressive in its characteristics. Even before the first petition had received consideration, another was submitted, in the name of a certain William Southeby, praying for the "*total* abolition of slavery in Pennsylvania." Both these measures, however, shared the fate of their predecessor and were canceled by the same transatlantic policy.

In 1715, a meeting was held, the avowed aim of which was to obtain a minute rendering unlawful any subsequent purchase

---

[1] *Col. Rec. of Pa.*, II, 402.

of slaves. For some reason or other, this Assembly failed to accomplish the object for which it had been convened. Some of the Quakers, however, did not require such a restraint. From conscientious scruples they refused to traffic in humanity. This fact is sufficiently well attested by a bit of correspondence, that has come down to posterity. In the same year, that is in 1715, one Jonathan Dickinson, a merchant of Philadelphia, writing to his correspondent in Jamaica, says, "I must entreat you to send me no more negroes for sale, for our people don't care to buy. They are generally against any coming into the country." In 1722, a further manifestation of the utter repugnance of the Society to negro slavery was made by an act of the Assembly imposing a high duty on the importation of blacks into the Province.

The Quakers had now commenced to have an abiding belief that slavery—"the selling of Joseph," "the root of bitterness," as it was variously termed—was inconsistent with the royal law of doing to others as we would have them do unto us. In their estimation, to subsist by the toil of those whom violence or cruelty had placed in their power was neither compatible with their profession as Christians, nor consistent with the mandates of common justice. They believed, moreover, that persistence in such an evil course would inevitably draw down the "displeasure of heaven" upon them.

John Woolman, describing a Southern tour made by him in the year 1746, declares, that "when I ate, drank, and lodged free of cost with people who lived in ease on the hard labor of their slaves, I felt uneasy; and as my mind was inward to the Lord, I found this uneasiness return upon me, at times, through the whole visit. Where the masters bore a good share of the burden, and lived frugally, so that their servants were well provided for, and their labor moderate, I felt more easy; but where they lived in a costly way, and laid heavy burdens on their slaves, my exercise was often great, and I frequently had conversation with them in private concerning it.[1] To him all slavery, no matter whether lenient or not, was a "dark gloominess hanging over the land."

Slavery, so thought most of the Friends, violated the Saviour's command, "Love one another as I have loved you." They raised the pertinent question, how can we be said to love our brethren while we bring, or for selfish ends, keep them in bondage? Do we act consistently with this noble principle when we impose such onerous burdens on our fellow creatures? The meetings were strongly of the opinion that they did not; hence the Friends were advised, and earnestly exhorted, to make the cause of the colored people their own. If slaves were born in their families they were entreated to "consider them as souls committed to your trust, whom the Lord will require at your hands."

Many of the Society, translating this advice into practice, did make the slave-cause their own. In 1722 the following notice was inserted in the *Mercury Gazette* of Pennsylvania: "A person, lately arrived, freely offers his services to teach his poor breathren, the male negroes, to read the Holy Scriptures, without any charge." This magnanimity was by no means unique in its character. There were many other incidents worthy to be placed by its side. Philanthropy was as much a distinguishing feature of the people of Pennsylvania in the days of Quaker supremacy as it has been at any time since that era.

The majority of the Friends remained constant in their determination not to import slaves, and, to prevent any member of the Society who might be so inclined from introducing them, the Yearly Meeting of 1755 declared that if any of its constituents bought or imported slaves the overseers should "speedily inform the Monthly Meeting of such trangressors, in order that the meeting may proceed to treat further with them, as they may be directed in the wisdom of Truth." This decision did not visit the extreme penalty of excommunication

---

[1] *Journal*, 72.

upon offenders, but it simply excluded them from the more select meetings; *i. e.,* those for discipline, and from the privilege of contributing to the pecuniary needs of the Society.

The resolution in its immediate operation appears to have produced little, if any, visible good. Some Quakers, of the liberal constructionist type, still persisted in participating in this traffic, and excuses of all sorts were freely urged in extenuation of their conduct. For example, the argument was frequently advanced that the wretchedness of the negroes, occasioned by their internecine wars, justified the whites in enslaving them; for, in so doing, they were actually improving the condition of the blacks, and thus performing a philanthropic work. But Woolman at once perceived that this specious plea was founded on an egregious misconception. He clearly pointed out that it was the eagerness with which slaves were purchased, and this circumstance alone that "animates these parties to push on the war, and increases desolation among them."[1]

At this juncture some of the slave-owning Friends declared that the negroes were the offspring of Cain, their blackness being the unmistakable mark God had stamped upon the race after its founder had so cruelly murdered his brother Abel; that it was the obvious design of Providence, therefore, that they should be slaves, as a condition proper to the tribe proceeding from an individual as desperately wicked as Cain certainly was. The other side was more than equal to the emergency. They contended, and that too on Scriptural authority, that the family of Noah were the only persons who survived the deluge; and as this Patriarch was of Seth's race, the descendants of Cain must have been utterly extirpated. The slave-owners were no sooner dislodged from this position than they entrenched themselves behind another Biblical argument. After the flood, said they, Ham went into the land of Nod and took a wife; this country was far distant, inhabited

---

[1] *Journal*, 104.

by Cain's race, and was not submerged by the deluge; as Ham was sentenced to be a servant of servants to his brethren, the issue of these two abominably wicked families was doubtless intended for the position of slaves—indeed, they were suitable for nothing else. This was certainly a most formidable array of Biblical arguments; but the language of Woolman soon controverted such line of reasoning. He boldly appealed to their own judgment. "The flood," contended he, "was a judgment upon the world for their wickedness, and it was granted that Cain's stock was the most wicked, and therefore unreasonable to suppose that they were spared."[1] Moreover, he reminded his brethren that the Scriptures positively assert that "all flesh died that moved upon the earth."

The minority perceived the props taken one by one from their tottering cause, but yet they declined to surrender. Affairs continued in this unsatisfactory state for some time, although with the majority of the Friends it was now war to the knife with the institution of slavery. Nothing but absolute abolition being considered compatible with their profession as Christians.

In the Yearly Meeting of Philadelphia in 1758, the subject of slavery was vehemently discussed. Woolman, the apostle of emancipation, was present on this occasion, and his language will be employed to describe the action taken. "Many faithful brethren," writes our author, "labored with great firmness, and the love of truth in a good degree prevailed. Several who had negroes expressed their desire that a rule might be made to deal with such Friends as offenders who bought slaves in the future. To this it was answered that the root of this evil should never be effectually struck at until a thorough search was made in the circumstances of such Friends as kept negroes, with respect to the righteousness of their motives in keeping them, that impartial justice might be administered throughout." "Several Friends," his

---

[1] *Journal*, 106.

account continues, "expressed their desire that a visit might be made to such Friends as kept slaves, and many others said that they believed liberty was the negroes' right; to which, at length, no opposition was publicly made."[1] In conclusion, the members of the Society were earnestly and affectionately entreated to "steadily observe the injunction of our Lord and Master, 'To do unto others, as we would they should do unto us;' which it now appears to this meeting, would induce such Friends who have any slaves to set them at liberty—making a Christian provision for them, according to their age."

Unfortunately, however, such benevolent opinions appeared very far from the creed of the recreant slave owners, who in direct opposition to the admonitions of both meetings and Friends, persisted in their pernicious ways. Consequently, the Quakers were compelled to resort to other expedients for the attainment of their object. The Friends, although never an exclusive sect in the strict sense of the word, had, up to this time, attempted no united effort. In a struggle of such paramount importance, however, the applicability of the old motto—In union there is strength—was evident. All religious predilections were to be temporarily banished, and the Society now proclaimed its perfect willingness to act in concert with all those, who, without reference to denominational belief, were, as regards this one cardinal topic, of the same faith and order.

In 1774, therefore, an alliance, offensive as well as defensive, was consummated with all such persons, in order to make a grander, and, as it was hoped, a more effectual effort for the suppression of this iniquity. It appears almost superfluous to add that the actuating cause of such combination was not to shift responsibility. The Quakers considered themselves relieved of no part of their obligation. True, they would urge others, but they would also labor unceasingly themselves. And measures more stringent in character

---

[1] *Journal*, pp. 137-8.

were soon directed against any of their congregation who should offend in this particular. About this time it was declared that all Quakers concerned in importing, selling, purchasing, transporting slaves in any possible way were to be excluded from membership; or, in the peculiar Society phrase, *disowned*.

The Quakers were commanded to shun even the appearances of evil. They were to abstain from any participation in slavery themselves, and were to pass a sort of non-intercourse act against those who, contrary to all admonitions, still persisted in such conduct. All Friends were earnestly cautioned and advised against acting as executors or administrators of estates where slaves were bequeathed or likely to be retained in servitude. They were not even to serve as scribes for such individuals, for by so doing they became instrumental, in a certain degree, in perpetuating bondage. Many are the recorded instances in which penmen, of the Quaker persuasion, absolutely refused to write such documents; and if they eventually complied with the request it was always under protest. The experience of John Woolman in this respect is only typical of a class. "My employer," such are his words, "having a negro woman, sold her, and desired me to write a bill of sale, the man being waiting who bought her. The thing was sudden, and, though the thought of writing an instrument of slavery for one of my fellow creatures made me feel uneasy, yet I remembered I was hired by the year, that it was my master who directed me to do it, and that it was an elderly man, a member of our Society, who bought her. So, through weakness I gave way and wrote, but, at executing it, I was so afflicted in my mind, that I said before my master and the Friend, that I believed slave-keeping to be a practice inconsistent with the Christian religion."

On another occasion, he informs us that an acquaintance desired him to draw up his last testament. "I knew," says Woolman, "he had slaves, and asking his brother, was told he intended to leave them as slaves to his children. As writing is a profitable employ, and as offending sober people was disagreeable to my inclination, I was straitened in my mind; but as I looked to the Lord, he inclined my heart to his testimony. I told the man that I believed the practice of continuing slavery to this people was not right, and that I had a scruple in my mind against doing writings of that kind; that though many in our Society kept them as slaves, still I was not easy to be concerned in it, and desired to be excused from going to write the will."[1] The friend expostulated in vain. Woolman remained loyal to his conscience. He declared it was perfectly clear to him that he "ought not to be the scribe where wills are drawn," by which human beings are continued in a life-long slavery. Here, as elsewhere, even the man who runs may read on the page of history, that, although self-interest has in many instances exercised despotic sway, altruism has not been altogether unknown.

In 1776, after much prayerful consideration, the Yearly Meeting took final action. A statute of excommunication was launched against every member who should longer detain a negro in a state of bondage. It was declared in the most unequivocal manner that "where any members continue to reject the advice of their brethren, and refuse to execute proper instruments of writing for releasing from a state of slavery such as are in their power, or to whom they have any claim, whether arrived to full age. or in their minority, and no hopes of the continuance of Friends' labor being profitable to them; that Monthly Meetings after having discharged a Christian duty to such, should testify their disunion with them." In accordance with this resolution, the subordinate meetings were directed to "deny the right of membership to such as persist in holding their fellow men as property." Thus the same year that the English Colonies in America declared themselves independent of Great Britain, the slaves of the Quakers in Pennsylvania were to be manumitted. But in the earnestness of the Society still more aggressive measures were to be taken. In 1778, another

---

[1] *Journal*, pp. 80-1.

injunction was added to the long list relating to slavery. It was then announced that all children of emancipated slaves should be tenderly advised, and that a suitable education should be freely provided for them.

The decree of absolute emancipation had now gone forth, but the complete abolition of slavery was not so speedily accomplished as some of the Friends in their eagerness desired. The reasons for the delay were many and various. Prominent among them was the fact that the slave owner, even if inclined to liberate his slaves, had many impediments besetting his path. Besides having to struggle against great pecuniary loss, he was compelled to contend with obstacles that the law imposed. To see the difficulty superimposed by legislation upon emancipation, we need only to turn the leaves of some of the colonial statute books. In Pennsylvania, where the law was probably the most favorable in this respect, the individuals liberating their slaves were obliged to enter into bond for the payment of £30, so as to provide for the possibility of the freedman becoming chargeable for maintenance.

As early as the year 1759, however, Woolman had said, "the case is difficult to some who have slaves, but if such set aside all self interest, and come to be weaned from the desire of getting estates, or even from holding them together, when truth requires the contrary, I believe way will so open that they will know how to steer through those difficulties."[1] True to his prophetic assertion, the way did open; or, to speak more accurately, the Quakers blazed out for themselves a path in this as yet untrodden forest. Notwithstanding all the pecuniary and legal obstructions that seemed to block the way, they could not be restrained from doing what they were convinced was morally right. Many manumitted their slaves without the slightest regard to possible consequences. Others, while performing the same meritorious action, afforded the most splendid illustrations of philanthropy. They not only consented to surrender their property—thereby incurring the pen-

---

[1] *Journal*, p. 136.

alties attending manumission—but they also calculated and gave (deducting the cost of food and clothing) what was due the slaves for wages from the beginning of their servitude to the very day when their liberation was declared. This was done in many instances. The case of Warner Mifflin, who paid all his adult slaves on their discharge the sum which arbitrators mutually chosen awarded them, may be selected as a concrete example.

While the Society was thus performing its duty to the slaves and free people of color within their jurisdiction, a desire began to awaken among its members for the extinction of slavery throughout the length and breadth of America. From this time on, formal memorials and remonstrances relative to this subject were repeatedly laid before persons placed in high authority as well as before the public at large. Petitions were frequently presented to Congress, and other legislative bodies, praying for the total suppression of this barbarity.[1] But the Quakers did not confine exclusively their exertions to such efforts. They went further. Not content with manumitting their own negroes, they even endeavored to liberate all the people of color that chanced to come within the boundaries of their State.

General Washington, writing from Mount Vernon under the date April 12, 1786, speaks of the case of a certain Mr. Dably, residing at Alexandria, whose slave had escaped to Philadelphia, and "whom a society of Quakers in the city, formed for such purposes, have attempted to liberate." From Mr. Dably's account of the occurrence, General Washington concluded "that this society is not only acting repugnantly to justice, so far as its conduct concerns strangers, but in my opinion impoliticly with respect to the State, the city in particular, without being able, except by acts of tyranny and oppression, to accomplish its own ends."[2] The expression of

---

[1] These efforts were not to go unrewarded. Influenced mainly by the unceasing endeavors of the Quakers, the Legislature of Pennsylvania passed an act abolishing slavery in the year 1780.

[2] Sparks, *Washington*, IX, 158.

such opinions, however, caused the Quakers little, if any, concern. They were firmly persuaded that even if their endeavors were not in strict conformity with human legislation that their conduct was approved by a higher, by a divine mandate, and this was of infinitely more importance to them.

The year 1778 marks the consummation of the struggle. At this time, as far as the author's reading extends, there was not a slave in the possession of an acknowledged Quaker within the confines of the State of Pennsylvania.

By way of recapitulation, it should be remarked that the obnoxious practice of slave-holding had apparently obtained a footing among the members of the Society before they awoke to a realization of the iniquity of the institution. Those of their number who had always been convinced of its sinfulness, never tired of declaiming against its unlawfulness and urging the utter repugnance of slavery to a high religious profession. But the enthusiasm of these social reformers was invariably tempered with Christian prudence and forbearance. Their method of procedure was always characterized by discretion as well as by perseverance. Persuasion constituted the only weapon employed against those whom they believed to be in error. Compulsion was never resorted to. Day after day, month after month, year after year, did they patiently exhort and labor with their wayward brethren who persisted in retaining their fellow creatures in a state of bondage. From first to last the abolitionists among the Friends sought by example and argument to induce the colonists, especially the members of their own denomination, to abstain from any participation in this traffic in humanity. Though often discouraged, they did not grow weary in well-doing, and in due season the harvest was reaped; for, after a lapse of nearly a century of uninterrupted endeavor, their efforts were crowned with glorious success. Then was secured the end after which they had striven so long and faithfully—the recognition that all men are by nature free and equal.

www.ingramcontent.com/pod-product-compliance
Lightning Source LLC
Chambersburg PA
CBHW031606110426
42742CB00037B/1299